The Rhetoric of
Doubtful Authority

The Rhetoric of
Doubtful Authority

DECONSTRUCTIVE READINGS OF
SELF-QUESTIONING NARRATIVES,
ST. AUGUSTINE TO FAULKNER

RALPH FLORES

Cornell University Press

ITHACA AND LONDON

First published 1984 by Cornell University Press.
Published in the United Kingdom by Cornell University Press Ltd.,
London.

International Standard Book Number 0-8014-1625-6
Library of Congress Catalog Card Number 83-15297
Printed in the United States of America
*Librarians: Library of Congress cataloging information
appears on the last page of the book.*

*The paper in this book is acid-free and meets the guidelines
for permanence and durability of the Committee on Production
Guidelines for Book Longevity of the Council on Library Resources.*

The term *auctores* was . . . applied to those from whom we derive title to property. *Auctor* certainly comes from *autos*, "*proprius*" or "*suus ipsius*."

The nations were governed by the certainty of authority, that is, by the same criterion which is used by our metaphysical criticism; namely, the common sense of the human race.
—Vico, *The New Science*

Contents

Preface

This book attempts to apply the techniques of deconstruction to a series of texts that have been more or less canonized, from century to century, as "great books" of the Western tradition. It begins with certain problems in the concepts of "rhetoric" and "authority," and relates those problems to aberrations such as the monster or outsider against—yet within—the normal or proper. It aims to demonstrate, through its readings, how the undoing of genealogical lines or of conventional humanism can be linked to certain techniques, and failures, of cultural power.

Since my endeavor is called deconstructive, something needs to be said about deconstruction, which is at times described as a strategy with several aspects: (1) the noticing of binary oppositions and their hierarchizing or totalizing effects, (2) the inversion and dismantling of the oppositions, (3) the preclusion of the emergence of a synthesizing term that would produce a new hierarchy or totalization.[1] We need not consider these three aspects to constitute a method. One of the oddities of deconstruction is indeed that since the aspects are strictly speaking neither phases in a sequence

[1] Jacques Derrida, *Positions* (Paris: Minuit, 1972), pp. 56–57. Here and elsewhere, when reference is given only to a foreign-language edition, the translation is mine.

9

nor part of a strategy that is teleological,[2] we can never be certain in any particular instance whether deconstruction operates as a critique, whether there is a deconstructor (as agent) at work, or whether a deconstruction has been completed or has even taken place.

For convenience, however, and because my readings will deal with texts that belong to philosophy as well as to literature, I would suggest a number of instances in which deconstruction—as critique—seems most clearly to occur: Jacques Derrida's reading of Husserl's *Ideas* (in *Speech and Phenomena*), of John Austin's *How to Do Things with Words* (in *Margins of Philosophy*), of Plato's *Phaedrus* (in *Dissemination*), and of Hegel's *Philosophy of Right* (in *Glas*).[3] These are texts that belong to what is conventionally called philosophy, and Derrida gives some indications—if rather indirectly—as to why the procedures of deconstruction might seem most visible in his reading of such texts: what is called philosophy is a discourse that believes "that it thinks its other," or that it can always appropriate to itself what is alien to it, that is, interiorize what is exterior.[4] The effort of deconstruction is not merely to oppose philosophy but to articulate some "other" that philosophy cannot appropriate or, paradoxically (in an image that will recur at the outset of Chapter 1), to penetrate or even puncture the philosopher's ear, which hears only what it will:

> Can one violently penetrate philosophy's field of listening without its immediately—even pretending in advance, by hearing what is said of it, by decoding the statement—making the penetration resonate within itself . . . ? In other words, can one

---

[2]*Ibid.*, p. 95.

[3]*Speech and Phenomena and Other Essays on Husserl's Theory of Signs*, trans. D. B. Allison (Evanston: Northwestern University Press, 1973); *Margins of Philosophy*, trans. A. Bass (Chicago: University of Chicago Press, 1982); *Dissemination*, trans. B. Johnson (Chicago: University of Chicago Press, 1981); *Glas* (Paris: Galilée, 1974).

[4]*Margins of Philosophy*, xiii.

puncture the tympanum of a philosopher and still be heard and understood by him [*continuer à se faire entendre de lui*]?[5]

If we are to make the philosopher hear, rather than become deaf, the violence against his ear cannot be frontal or symmetrical, for any such opposition would be welcomed as dialectics. The violence must be perforce indirect, sly, and in a certain sense rhetorical, for it questions (in) the margin by which philosophy would insulate and define itself.

At some such point of alterity to philosophy we might venture to locate texts called "literary," if only this were not to treat as clear-cut the margins under contestation. To reformulate the problem: texts called philosophical and those called literary, to the extent that both name or delimit themselves as such, make a similar gesture; thus each can be similarly interrogated beyond its meaning or theme, that is, "as a determined text inscribed in a general text, enclosed in the representation of its own margin."[6]

This much having been said, however, we might note that the texts called "literary" usually (but not always) have been open to that "general text"—a pervasiveness of textuality —or to an effacing or transgression of their margins. Such is especially the case with the texts that I shall designate, in the chapters to come, as "self-questioning." The quality of literariness in such texts, irrespective of their conventional genres, might be described as a certain fictiveness (events or identities neither present nor absent) akin to the play of *différance*, that is, "of a trace which no longer belongs to the horizon of Being, but whose play transports and encloses the meaning of Being."[7] Texts marked by such literariness are

---

[5]*Ibid.*, p. xii; *Marges de la philosophie* (Paris: Minuit, 1972), p. iii.

[6]*Margins*, p. xxiii.

[7]*Margins*, p. 22. "Différance" is a term coined to point to the impossible (non-)origin of difference in differing-deferring: "In a language, in the *system* of language, there are only differences. . . . On the one hand, these differences *play*: in language, in speech too, and in the exchange between language and speech. On the other hand, these differences are themselves

those which are likely to seem already deconstructed or which anticipate the deconstructionist commentator, who is thus left with little to do.

Just so, some of Derrida's readings—of, say, Artaud, Mallarmé, or Valéry—are not deconstructive, or at least not actively or critically so;[8] he mostly notes the dismantlings they have already implemented (acknowledging for example that Valéry "recognized the immense bearing of [the] autonomous circuit of 'hearing-oneself-speak' . . . and did so better, without a doubt, than any traditional philosopher").[9] We are, even so, hardly able to postulate some sort of distinction between philosophical (or active) and literary (or passive) deconstruction, precisely because such oppositions must themselves, in at least two general ways, be put into question. First, "logocentrism"[10] is culturally ubiquitous; it is by no means limited to philosophy or literature or religion but is the most basic resource for our making sense, emotionally and intellectually, of the discourses of our culture. All literary texts allow themselves to be read—in varying degrees and often by way of long detours—logocentrically; nor is

---

effects. They have not fallen from the sky fully formed. . . . What is written as *différance* will be the playing movement that 'produces'—by means of something that is not simply an activity—these differences, these effects of difference" (*Margins*, p. 11). As for the term "literariness," its use here overlaps with that of the Russian formalists when they point to "defamiliarization" (*ostranenie*). Far from establishing a purpose or essence of literature, however, the term here suggests that there is no "being-literary" or "literary-being" of literature (see *Dissemination*, p. 223).

[8]The readings appear, respectively, in *Writing and Difference*, trans. A. Bass (Chicago: University of Chicago Press, 1978), pp. 169–95, 232–50; *Dissemination*, pp. 175–285; *Margins*, pp. 275–306. For doubts about whether such readings are deconstructive, see Jonathan Culler, *On Deconstruction: Theory and Criticism after Structuralism* (Ithaca: Cornell University Press, 1982), p. 213, and Samuel Weber, "After 8: Remarking *Glyph*," in *Glyph 8* (Baltimore: Johns Hopkins University Press, 1981), p. 234.

[9]*Margins*, p. 287.

[10]"Logocentrism" is complicitous with metaphysics and assumes the priority of voice or consciousness over writing, identity over distance or difference; see *Of Grammatology*, trans. G. Spivak (Baltimore: Johns Hopkins University Press, 1976), p. 12.

logocentrism incompatible with deconstruction, since each is a setup for the other. My only quarrel, in the pages to follow, is with commentaries that ignore those settings up and would shorten or bypass the detours. Second, even where we might feel justified in believing that an obvious deconstruction is going on, it can never be easily specified as a passive or active commentary working against, or coming from, any particular author.[11] Part of the thrust of deconstruction is that it must turn, as in Derrida's reading of Plato's *Phaedrus*, against its own possibly critical results: "It would be impossible to say to what extent [Plato] manipulates [the chain of significations connected with *pharmakon*] voluntarily or consciously, and at what point he is subject to the constraints weighing on his discourse from 'language.'"[12] Any urge to specify such a point is always subject to a series of interrogations that must themselves be interrogated:

> Plato can *not* see the links [*liaisons*], can leave them in the shadow or break them up [*les y interrompre*]. And yet these links go on working of themselves. In spite of him? thanks to him? in *his* text? *outside* his text? but then where? between his text and the language? for what reader? at what moment? . . . There is some malformation in the question.[13]

There can be no end, it seems, to the requestioning of questions.

Yet, to recapitulate, if neither the authors nor the subjects nor the activity of deconstruction can be located, the force of critique is not on that account lessened but may on the contrary suggest habits so chronic and addictive as to require enormous and unending exertions. If, again, Derrida's read-

[11]We might recall at this point that "that which lets itself be designated *différance* is neither simply active nor simply passive, announcing or rather recalling something like the middle voice, saying an operation that is not an operation, an operation that cannot be conceived either as passion or as the action of a subject on an object" (*Margins*, p. 9).

[12]*Dissemination*, p. 129.

[13]*Dissemination*, p. 96; *La dissémination* (Paris: Seuil, 1972), p. 108.

ings of philosophy are more perspicuous than his readings of literature, this hardly can be used to inscribe a boundary between different sorts of deconstruction. For philosophy is tied to a pervasive system of authority and rhetoric, both of which are hollowed out by diacritical otherness. My endeavor indeed will be to pay attention to that otherness, or more specifically, to the monstrousness in or of the normal or proper, that is, in a series of texts crucial to the Western tradition which nonetheless doubt their relation to that tradition. Whether or not the endeavor turns out to be relentlessly deconstructive is probably less important than that it move toward a noticing of the blindnesses required for our ideas of "humanism" and "tradition."

What becomes, one might ask, of the humanistic tradition when read in such a way? The question may prove difficult since, as will become apparent, precisely the notion of *traditio*, of an authoritative handing down from generation to generation, will be part of what is under scrutiny. The opening chapter poses the question of questions, in conjunction with rhetoric and authority, as a matter of aberration. Subsequent chapters implement the questioning in a reading of Augustinian allegory as an attempt to domesticate monstrosity and of Cartesian method as an unmaking of the self in its very desire for self-making. Such readings set the scene for others in which the notable figures turn out to be intriguingly, perhaps irremediably, aberrant. And so we may never be quite sure how marginal the readings of these texts and of our tradition, taken together, may appear to be.

The chapters to follow have undergone many metamorphoses, and my debts are many. I am grateful to several people (without suggesting that they necessarily subscribe to what I say) for reading various versions or parts, some now fortunately discarded, of this book: Ralph Freedman, Joseph Frank, Angel Flores, Maria Tatar, Alexander Gelley,

Preface

Harold Toliver, Murray Krieger, Patricia Tobin, Edward W. Said, Donald Pease, Paul de Man, Diana S. Goodrich, and Jonathan Culler. Earlier versions of some of the chapters have appeared in journals whose editors I thank for permission to reprint: Chapters 2 and 4 in the *New Orleans Review* 8, no. 3 (1981), and 10, no. 3 (1983), Chapter 3 in *SubStance* 39 (1983), and Chapter 6 in the *Structuralist Review* 5 (1983).

R<small>ALPH</small> F<small>LORES</small>

The Rhetoric of
Doubtful Authority

1

Questioning the
Question of Authority

quaero, to seek with longing, to miss, want; to seek to know, to ask, to inquire; to investigate.

quaesitio, an interrogation (by torture).

quaestor, in plur., the quaestors, magistrates in Rome. Of these, some tried criminal cases in the courts, or prosecuted at such trials; others accompanied consuls and praetors on military expeditions.

—*Cassell's New Latin Dictionary*

The question mark is graphically shaped; it resembles an ear. Usually passive and unnoticed, the ear may suddenly intrude itself: asking must be attended by a close listening, and listening, if unsatisfied, may multiply marks of ears. Shakespeare's *Hamlet*, just so, starts with a question ("Who's there?") and is interrogative throughout, particularly about King Hamlet's killing, which was accomplished through the ear.[1] At the play's beginning, an ear-poisoner has displaced, apparently with full success, a legitimate king and husband, and he announces his regal succession in the lovely rhetoric of balanced antitheses.[2] The antitheses bring together in apparent harmony ("with dirge in marriage and mirth in funeral") the oppositions of a kingdom to which the king, as self-styled healer, proposes to minister. Although ut-

[1] See Harry Levin, *The Question of Hamlet* (New York: Oxford University Press, 1959), and, on ear-poisoning, Sigurd Burckhardt, *Shakespearean Meanings* (Princeton: Princeton University Press, 1968), p. 269.

[2] *Hamlet*, ed. C. Hoy (New York: Norton, 1963), I.ii.1–39.

19

terly questionable, if at this point only to Hamlet, the announcement comes utterly without questions, and the ear-
poisoner continues his ruinous deed publicly, though still
perilously. He continues, in other words, to pour something
into the ear of Denmark: knowing about ears, he is able to
mime—with an ease that should seem outrageous—the very
voice of legitimate rulership.

The situation might give us pause, as it indeed gives pause
to the prince. For how can authority, poisoning or poisoned,
be questioned? Any contestation is not necessarily a matter
of truth against falsity or of strength against weakness, for
the marks and acts of questioning are signs that by definition
are inconclusive. The situation is inscribed, indeed, at the
script's most literal level: the poisoned father designated as
"Ghost" is doubled in the name ("Hamlet") with the son almost similarly ineffective, while the usurping brother, never
named as Claudius (except in the *dramatis personae*), is designated throughout the play—and after all, correctly—as
"King." The ostensibly true but now prior king can appear
only as something insubstantial and spectral—a "figure" or
"image." He is in a "questionable shape," and he astonishingly (and not quite credibly) doubles or "usurp[s]" the
king's "fair and warlike form."[3] Again, the ensuing noctur-
nal exchange between the two Hamlets, with its plethora of
exclamation marks (so like question marks), is extraordinary
to the point of uselessness and results mostly in the prince's
famous deferrals, doubts, errors, and questions.

Questions are prominent, of course, not only in *Hamlet* but
in other texts of the time, associated with such names as
Montaigne, Machiavelli, Luther, and Descartes. Questioning
became frequent and disruptive, and the question of questions was the authority of questioning *as* the questioning of
authority. "Authority" and "questioning" (or what Edward

[3]*Ibid.*, I.i.41, I.i.81, I.iv.43, I.i.47.

W. Said aptly calls "molestation"[4]), even or especially when thought of as oppositional terms, were curiously intertwined with each other, and it was never clear which served or mastered which. We need hardly rehearse, for instance, the paradox of the Reformation as both an attack and a defense of traditional Christianity. If external ecclesiastical authorities were suspect, was internal conscience any less so? If certainty of conscience was sanctioned when divinely guaranteed, who could be certain of having that guarantee? When Miguel Servetus interpreted Scripture according to his conscience, finding in it no evidence for the Trinity, he was executed as a heretic by the Calvinists. Yet why would Servetus (as his defender Sebastian Castellio was to wonder) die in order to affirm an evident falsehood? Witchcraft and demonism could be adduced as supposed factors, but how judge those in turn? Given the subversive capacity of witches and demons, might not any judgment upon them be influenced by possible complicity with them?[5]

I

Such a plight, despite mention of specific epochs, "modern" or Roman, cannot be assigned a historical beginning. Notice, to recall this chapter's epigraphs, how *quaero*, as desire or longing, is tied to *quaesitio* as torture or *quaestor* as prosecuting magistrate. The question mark looks like a hook

---

[4]*Beginnings: Intention and Method* (New York: Basic, 1975), pp. 81–100. Consider especially the following: "No novelist has ever been unaware that his authority, regardless of how complete, or the authority of a narrator, is a sham. Molestation . . . is a consciousness of one's duplicity, one's confinement to a fictive, scriptive realm" (p. 84). Said's formulations are astute and helpful, and the emphasis here differs only slightly: I would extend somewhat the conception of secondariness to other and prior texts than novels and would stress that "molestation" is not only an opposite or undoing of authority but a necessary aspect of it.

[5]Richard H. Popkin, *The History of Scepticism from Erasmus to Descartes* (New York: Harper & Row, 1968), pp. 6–13, 185.

as well as an ear; it catches or latches or baits, so as to elicit what otherwise might not be said. But questioning, like fishing, depends partly on mere luck, and as an aspect of authority it may signal, we might speculate, some telling vulnerability.

The concept of *auctoritas* has, after all, the feel of secondariness: it denotes a supplementation by senatorial elders of a projected course of action. The *auctor* offers "more than advice but less than command,"[6] almost as if trying to become the *archē* he never is. By definition he augments, guiding but not controlling the development of any putative offspring. Ideally a public *auctor* connects present communal values with a shared past and future, but his work is implicitly doubtful because it merely points. We may thus be suspicious of claims such as Hannah Arendt's that authority in its presumably "genuine" form stood behind Rome's imperial stability and that it was not what it was later confused with—power (or violence) and persuasion: "Authority precludes the use of external means of coercion; where force is used, authority itself has failed. Authority, on the other hand, is incompatible with persuasion, which presupposes equality and works through a process of argumentation."[7] This description is riddled with difficulties and (incidentally) is totally at odds with that of Giambattista Vico, whose *auctores* held their rights by violence and terrifying persuasion. Can there be purely non-"external" coercion, or can an *auctor* authorize without even a scintilla of rhetoric? Whether authority became impure, however, or was always impure to begin with, it demarks efforts—so I shall speak of it

[6]Carl J. Friedrich, "Authority, Reason and Discretion," in *Authority*, ed. C. J. Friedrich (Cambridge: Harvard University Press, 1958). On authority, see also Max Horkheimer, *Critical Theory*, trans. M. O'Connell et al. (New York: Herder, 1972), pp. 68–127; *From Max Weber*, ed. H. Gerth and C. W. Mills (New York: Oxford University Press, 1946), pp. 295–302.

[7]"What Is Authority?" in *Between Past and Future: Six Exercises in Political Thought* (Cleveland: World, 1961), p. 93.

here—of supplementing and broaching, efforts valorized by oppositions and constituted by force. As a pointing, *auctoritas* is semiotic, its discourse ambiguously giving and needing, like a question, *energeia*, or the power of language traditionally designated, somewhat vaguely, as "rhetorical."

This rhetorical aspect is not immediately apparent, and it may lead to problems. For if rhetoric seems to insert itself into both "authority" and "question," it does so in a two-faced and doubtful manner: an "argument from authority," however effective as persuasion, is classified often and openly as a fallacy, while a "rhetorical question" is meant to be taken seriously not as a question but as an assertion.[8] The nonrhetorical question or *interrogatio*, by alleged contrast, has a serious, even violent, intent: a skillful advocate, Quintilian observes, can make questions seem accusatory and may force witnesses into inconsistencies.[9] Is *interrogatio*, even so, any less "rhetorical" than rhetorical questioning? The rhetorical question, in not asking what it asks, is marked by desire, that is, by assertion and irony or risk; but so too are supposedly nonfigurative questions, which must imply or sometimes brutally state assertions precisely in order to frame and direct a reply.

In either case, interrogative force depends on not questioning the question, and we may wonder about the figurative/nonfigurative distinction by which deviations can be properly deviant, for only by a presupposition whose figurality is concealed or smoothed away with usage can rhetorical questions or other figures seem to be separated from their supposedly nonfigurative counterparts.[10] A recognition of this presupposition is precisely what should come

---

[8]Pierre Fontanier, *Les figures du discours* (1821–30; repr. Paris: Flammarion, 1968), pp. 368–70.

[9]*Institutio Oratoria*, vol. 2, trans. H. E. Butler, Loeb ed. (Cambridge: Harvard University Press, 1939), V.vii.27–30.

[10]See Jacques Derrida, "White Mythology," trans. F. T. C. Moore, *NLH* 4 (1974):5–74.

most easily—and so may most quickly be denied—by the theorists of rhetoric. My effort, in the chapters to follow, might be called transrhetorical, or a persistent putting into question of questioning itself. The stakes may well be considerable, since if questions make presumptions about what they question, a questioning of questions can at some point start a dismantling of rhetoric, including literary rhetoric, and (or as) the enterprise of metaphysics.

In its possible role as an untrustworthy double agent or supplement of metaphysics, rhetoric has had a somewhat elusive status. Though often the sign and instrument of leadership and wisdom, rhetoric in the West has as often been relegated (with questionable success) to a socially secondary or "outside" position.[11] It is detested at times as too verbose and at others—sometimes indistinguishably—as too insidious; recall Gorgias of Leontini contending that "1) Nothing exists, 2) if anything exists it is incomprehensible, 3) if it is comprehensible, it is incommunicable."[12] The implication is a disjunction—the *logos* is freed from mimetic adherence to "reality" but still is exploitable as persuasion.[13] "Reality" or referentiality is suspended in favor of figurality, and we will notice what might be called rhetoricity, in what follows, as rhetoric's unlimited side, when gaps become wa-

[11]For a few typically troubled moments in rhetoric's past, see Jacqueline de Romilly, *Magic and Rhetoric in Greece* (Cambridge: Harvard University Press, 1975); Nancy Streuver, *The Language of History in the Renaissance* (Princeton: Princeton University Press, 1970); Walter J. Ong, *Rhetoric, Romance and Technology* (Ithaca: Cornell University Press, 1971), chap. 1; Richard M. Weaver, *The Ethics of Rhetoric* (Chicago: Regnery, 1965), chaps. 1, 7; Kenneth Burke, *Counter-Statement* (1931; repr. Berkeley: University of California Press, 1968); the attack on Burke by Wilbur S. Howell in "Kenneth Burke's 'Lexicon Rhetoricae': A Critical Examination," reprinted in *Poetics, Rhetoric and Logic: Studies in the Basic Disciplines of Criticism* (Ithaca: Cornell University Press, 1975) pp. 234–55; Burke's response to Howell in *Language as Symbolic Action* (Berkeley: University of California Press, 1966), pp. 304–7.
[12]*The Pre-Socratic Philosophers*, ed. K. Freeman (Oxford: Blackwell, 1946), p. 359.
[13]Charles P. Segal, "Gorgias and the Psychology of the *Logos*," *Harvard Studies in Philology* 66 (1962):112.

vering drives for so-called communication even as the strong accompanying terror is a taboo against communicative misengendering: "rhetoric," says I. A. Richards, "should be a study of misunderstanding and its remedies."[14] The remedies *of* rhetoric, however, may also have to be remedies *for* it; they are undecidably medicines or poisons, as Jacques Derrida shows in a reading of Plato,[15] and what rhetoric can or should be may always become, however rhetorically, a question.

The "being" of metaphysics can be questioned by pointing to figurality, that is, to the reversibility or substitutability of supposedly fixed hierarchical oppositions such as true and false, cause and effect, subject and object, outside and inside. As recent theoreticians such as Philippe Lacoue-Labarthe and Paul de Man have shown, Friedrich Nietzsche's devastating revaluation of Western thinking proceeds, not without radical dislocations of his own discourse, as a series of deconstructions that can be related to his early lectures on rhetorical figures.[16] The revaluation cannot be described as a discovery of contradictions, since the Aristotelian principle of noncontradiction owes its persuasiveness, Nietzsche in effect argues, to the substitution of metaphoric for metonymic connections (that is, of figures which assemble or integrate polarities on the basis of analogy for figures which reverse or scramble such polarities on the basis of contingency or contiguity); nor can "doing" or "performance," with its implied agents or authors, possibly replace, as we might be tempted to assume, what had been called knowing or truth. The Nietzschean critique of metaphysics would have to be

[14]*The Philosophy of Rhetoric* (1935; repr. New York: Oxford University Press, 1964), p. 3.

[15]*La dissémination* (Paris: Seuil, 1972), pp. 69–179.

[16]Philippe Lacoue-Labarthe, "Le détour (Nietzsche et la rhétorique)," *Poétique* 2 (1971):53–76; Paul de Man, *Allegories of Reading: Figural Language in Rousseau, Nietzsche, Rilke, and Proust* (New Haven: Yale University Press, 1979), pp. 79–131.

described, to borrow de Man's phrasing, as "the deconstruction of the illusion that the language of truth (*episteme*) could be replaced by a language of persuasion (*doxa*)."[17] Texts called "philosophical" or "rhetorical" cannot, any more than those called "literary," be freed from the necessities and errors of figurality. Incompatible figurations, however, can be staged and read in varying ways—for instance, in the disruptions of metaphoric claims made metonymically or in the tensions between a text's implied metalinguistic statements and its rhetorical praxis.[18]

The "self-questioning narratives" of my subtitle may be described as those which thematize such tensions and disruptions, and which might be classed, in their self-reflexivity, as "Augustinian" or (more familiarly) as "Cartesian." Recent writers especially seem to write about writing; novelists, for instance, perform a "laying bare" of devices, a display of backstage authorial machinery, an insistence that telling is, quintessentially, about telling itself. Novels of novel making are everywhere, and prominent instances are readily at hand: Rilke's *Malte Laurids Brigge*, Proust's *Recherche*, Gide's *Counterfeiters*, Nabokov's *Pale Fire*, Beckett's trilogy.

To gauge what is at stake, we can allow straightaway that some sorts of self-questioning are perennial—in the stories, say, of Orpheus, Narcissus, or Oedipus. But precisely by recalling such myths we might characterize more recent self-questioning narratives as those which question (1) the "self" or "psychology," (2) the text's world or author or narrator or producer (implicitly, the reader or reading), or (3) the workings of stories and, indeed, of any "significant" discourse. Like theoreticians who disparage or dislocate the subject in favor of writing or codes,[19] self-questioning writers ironize

[17]De Man, *Allegories of Reading*, p. 130.
[18]*Ibid.*, pp. 14–18, 98–99.
[19]Friedrich Nietzsche, *Beyond Good and Evil*, trans. R. J. Hollingdale (Baltimore: Penguin, 1973), aphorisms 16–17; *The Will to Power*, trans. W. Kaufmann and R. J. Hollingdale (New York: Random House, 1967), apho-

the *auctor*-artist and his usual productions—the history or heroism that for centuries had been narrative's very stuff. My argument—at this point at its simplest—is that traditional or authorless myths, to the extent that they are believed to bespeak a privileged cosmic center, exercise relatively strong authority over their cultures,[20] but that narratives that break from mythic patterns to become self-questioning exert a far more doubtful authority. Since this formulation is merely tentative, one might place alongside the binary mythic/self-questioning the binary historical/modern. Modernity can be linked with a desire to wipe out the past, thus allowing for new departures, and modern writing struggles to displace the history without which its struggle could not be conceived.[21] The situation is afflictive, for such writing both affirms and negates its authority.

Few texts exemplify this situation more obviously than those of Descartes, whose position in Western history is itself curiously Cartesian. G. W. F. Hegel, for instance, seems to pause in his *Lectures on the History of Philosophy*: "With [Descartes] we genuinely enter into a self-sufficient philosophy, one which knows that . . . self-consciousness is an essential element of the true. Here, we can say, we are at home, and like the mariner after long wanderings on tumultuous seas, we can cry 'Land.' . . . With Descartes begins the development and thought of modern times [*anhebt die Bildung und Gedanken der neueren Zeit*]."[22] Hegel thus celebrates Des-

risms 482, 556; Michel Foucault, "What Is an Author?" in J. V. Harari, ed., *Textual Strategies* (Ithaca: Cornell University Press, 1979), pp. 141–60; Jacques Lacan, "The Subversion of the Subject and the Dialectic of Desire in the Freudian Unconscious," in *Ecrits*, trans. A. Sheridan (New York: Norton, 1977), pp. 292–325; Roland Barthes, "The Death of the Author," in *Image-Music-Text*, trans. S. Heath (New York: Hill & Wang, 1977), pp. 142–48.

[20]See Mircea Eliade, *Cosmos and History: The Myth of the Eternal Return* (New York: Harper & Row, 1953).

[21]Paul de Man, *Blindness and Insight: Essays in the Rhetoric of Contemporary Criticism* (New York: Oxford University Press, 1971), pp. 149–50.

[22]*Werke in Zwanzig Bänden*, vol. 3 (Frankfurt: Suhrkamp, 1971), p. 120.

cartes's self-consciousness as a precursor, possibly, to his own *Geist* in its movement toward self-recognition. Yet the paradox is that "home" is needed and can be imagined only when it is dispossessed or left behind:[23] we cannot know, despite reassurances, whether we will reach the land, whether that land was ever ours, or whether we are really in sight of land at all. What Descartes above all teaches, though mostly despite himself, is that self-consciousness as home is never quite at home, that self-exposure can never be entirely revealing, that self-consciousness is continually self-displacing.

This condition is domesticated (made at home) in our histories, which depict a conflict between the Cogito (internal or present) and authority (external or past): "The primary theme of the transition . . . to modern philosophy is the separation of reason from faith, the increasing freedom of man and his mind from the authority of tradition, . . . [the] loss of the solidarity of medieval man with the world of his past."[24] Do the oppositions here, we might ask, by which the West typically explains itself to itself, differ definitively from one another? Do they together exhaust the field of possibilities? It seems, on the contrary, that the Cartesian text marks a rupture precisely because such oppositional terms encroach upon each other's territories: freedom, consciousness, and self become newly authoritative, but always defen-

[23]See Georges Van den Abbeele, "Sightseers: The Tourist as Theorist," *Diacritics* 10, no. 4 (1980):9; more generally, Eric J. Sundquist, *Home as Found: Authority and Genealogy in Nineteenth-Century American Literature* (Baltimore: Johns Hopkins University Press, 1979). César du Marsais uses "borrowed home," we might notice, as a metaphor for all metaphors: "a word metaphorically is used in some sense other than its proper sense: 'it dwells in a borrowed home.'" Derrida, citing this passage, comments on metaphor so defined: "it is outside itself—it is itself, . . . a detour in (or in view of) the reappropriation, the self-presence of the idea" ("White Mythology," p. 55).

[24]Francis H. Parker, *The Story of Western Philosophy* (Bloomington: Indiana University Press, 1967), p. 174; also Sterling P. Lamprecht, *Our Philosophical Traditions* (New York: Appleton-Century-Crofts, 1955), pp. 209–10.

sively, in dubious countenancing of hypothetical demons amid a glaring, even blinding, "natural light." Not only does the Cogito belie the assurance it must constantly arrogate, but its movement as a contestation of authority is, despite contrary suggestions, the very gesture by which authority is most characteristically designated: an *auctor* founds the new at a necessary remove from the founding act itself.

The Cartesian gesture even in its defensive assertiveness has a certain appeal, because perplexities about "outside" referentiality (connected as it is with the authority of the "real" world and community) are set aside or else re-presented after an "inside" confrontation with immediate consciousness has supposedly shown that there, at least, representation is possible. This movement, which seems to permit some sort of appropriation, however limited, of an "outside" by an "inside," becomes a persistent if nonetheless misleading metaphor for reading (which gets "inside" a text so as to know the "outside" world or author) as practiced by even the most sophisticated of contemporary critics, with their recurrent dreams of uniting somehow the formalistic "inside" of literary texts with the "outside" of social fact.[25] And even when the dreams are not quite so encompassing, the Cartesian model still has pertinence, since recent movements to question (and others to assert) the "self" can be seen inevitably to involve a certain articulation of representational problems. Between the overture and accomplishment of logocentrism, Derrida claims, the motif of presence undergoes a modification, perhaps most conspicuously in the Cartesian Cogito: "Before that, the identity of presence offered to the mastery of repetition was constituted under the 'objective' form of the ideality of the *eidos* or the substantiality of *ousia*. Thereafter, this objectivity takes the form of *representation*, of the *idea* as the modification of a self-present substance, conscious and certain of itself at the moment of its relationship

[25]De Man, *Allegories of Reading*, pp. 3–19.

29

to itself."[26] This moment is transitory in Descartes's *Meditations*, and we can wonder how and with what consequences "Descartes had driven out the sign."[27] Does his violence toward that which "he excluded more violently than others"[28] turn out to be rhetorical—or less than successfully representational—even in precluding rhetoric?

The question is by no means limited to the Cartesian text: "the whole of modern metaphysics," writes Martin Heidegger, "maintains itself within Descartes's pioneering explication [*angebahnten Auslegung*]" of existents and truth; our anthropology—our cultural politics, our setting aside of philosophical questions—"cannot overcome Descartes, nor even rise up against him."[29] Even in our sense of some "crisis" of our epoch (and Descartes begins with such a sense), we are quite unable to locate a perspective from which to‘ think what is happening. Nihilism, writes Heidegger regarding Nietzsche, is the fundamental event of Western history—indeed, its "inner logic."[30] We are only beginning to understand this, and to notice that the place markers of our tradition (sun, horizon, sea) can no longer function as credible topoi, but only as metaphors for metaphoricity.

> The whole field of vision has been wiped away. The whole of that which is as such, the sea, has been drunk up by man. For man has risen up into [*ist aufgestanden in*] the I-ness of the *ego cogito*. Through this uprising, all that is, is transformed into object. That which is as the objective is swallowed up into the immanence of subjectivity. The horizon no longer emits light of itself. It is now nothing but the point-of-view posited in the value-positing of the will to power.[31]

[26]*Of Grammatology*, trans. G. Spivak (Baltimore: Johns Hopkins University Press, 1976), p. 97; Derrida's emphasis.
[27]*Ibid.*, p. 98.
[28]*Ibid.*
[29]Martin Heidegger, "The Age of the World Picture," in *The Question Concerning Technology and Other Essays*, trans. W. Lovitt (New York: Harper & Row, 1977), pp. 127, 140 (*Holzwege* [Frankfurt: Klostermann, 1963], p. 80).
[30]Heidegger, *Question*, p. 67.
[31]*Ibid.*, p. 107 (*Holzwege*, p. 241).

Questioning the Question of Authority

In this uprising neither subject nor object is left, and no sea, no sun. Yet this itself is a description marked by a certain ambiguity, and we may be reminded of Wallace Stevens's *Esthétique du Mal*:

> Reality explained.
> It was the last nostalgia: that he
> Should understand.

If the last nostalgia is an ability or hope to understand, must not some understanding, if only of the nostalgia itself, still go on? And if reality is left, though inexplicable, might not new eyes perhaps be required for it, or new stories?

II

With just such questions Cartesian writers have scanned the horizon of metaphors and sought somehow to refound foundations. Jean-Paul Sartre, even in his objections to Edmund Husserl's neo-Cartesian tactics, was as indebted as Husserl to Descartes; as he at one point indicates, "*Chez nous* [in our home; among us French], only one person has affected my mind: Descartes. I place myself in his lineage."[32] This is impressive, but can the placement of oneself in a lineage be quite so willed and conscious an act? Sartre and Husserl may be deemed Cartesians, indeed, in believing so confidently in their capacity to discriminate among which elements in their traditions to perpetuate—the most crucial element being consciousness itself, as undisturbed as possible by alterity, by signs, by resistances. If signs are undecidably other, however, we may be unable to master our representations; who, in that case, can be a singular writing agent, and by what authority?

Such a question is pertinent to the notion of communica-

[32]Quoted in Dominick LaCapra, *A Preface to Sartre* (Ithaca: Cornell University Press, 1978), p. 51; the critique of Husserl is in *Transcendence of the Ego*, trans. F. Williams and R. Kirkpatrick (New York: Farrar, Straus and Giroux, 1957).

tion (which is the subject of rhetoric) not only between persons face to face but between generations in a tradition. Husserl postulates a "European crisis" as a failure in transmitting the Renaissance ideal of unified knowledge, and he proposes that a phenomenological *Reaktivierung* is needed to recuperate apodictic aspects of the earlier life-world, thereby making them present, then and now, as a common structure.[33] Set against the sense of crisis, we are to believe, is the possibility of an unimpeded transmission through the centuries of "the same" meaning.

This ideal of communication is associable with a theory of signs that Derrida deconstructs,[34] along with the notion of "crisis." The Derridean project, however, which I shall frequently notice in the pages to follow, must itself be warily situated regarding the tradition that it calls into question. The space, Derrida writes, "between the overture and the philosophical accomplishment of phonologism (or logocentrism)" is not to be construed as history in some single sense, and the usual notion of a modern crisis is suspect "by virtue of what ties it to a dialectical and teleological determination of negativity."[35] Might not a questioning of the concept of history, however, even while locating a "rupture" primarily in "our epoch" (a typically modern tactic) obscure the quality, or epochality, of prior ruptures? Derrida, except for his readings of Plato and Aristotle, tends to privilege figures such as Novalis, Mallarmé, and a handful of avant-garde French writers—Artaud, Sollers, Bataille—whose "texts effect in their very movement the manifestation and practical deconstruction of a commonly accepted *representation* of literature."[36] While going on to concede that some texts "well

[33]*The Crisis of European Sciences and Transcendental Phenomenology*, trans. D. Carr (Evanston: Northwestern University Press, 1970).
[34]*Speech and Phenomena*, trans. D. Allison (Evanston: Northwestern University Press, 1973).
[35]*Of Grammatology*, pp. 97, 40.
[36]*Positions* (Paris: Minuit, 1972); Eng. trans. in *Diacritics* 3, no. 1 (1973):37.

before" these could have resisted models, Derrida offers no instances. Much literature, even so, might have been cited as disrupting the model or "representation" of literature—the texts, for example, of Ovid, Cervantes, Montaigne, or Boccaccio. Although such texts are by no means equally subversive of logocentrism, they might lead us to wonder whether the event of rupture—or of "our epoch"—can be bounded, even approximately, by the texts of Nietzsche, Freud, and Heidegger.

What I attempt here, however, is neither simply to recuperate nor simply to interrogate aspects of Western culture that Derrida might have neglected. On the contrary, "logocentrism" and "deconstruction" are not binary oppositions, nor can the first be construed as a "monolithic" tradition that the second merely puts into question.[37] The logocentric tradition cannot be described as monolithic, since deconstructive fissurings are always already apparent.

A point of possible confusion, though, may be Derrida's apparent privileging not only of modernism but, despite qualifications,[38] of a certain sense of "philosophy." Although his style relies at times on such "literary" devices as wordplay and fractured syntax, a certain bias may seem to emerge in an armory of terms that are technically both necessary and precise. Deconstruction is performed with the breaking up of conceptual oppositions followed by an unbalanced-unbalancing "double writing" that marks "the gap between the inversion which brings down the superior

[37]See Frank Lentricchia, *After the New Criticism* (Chicago: University of Chicago Press, 1980), p. 176: "The effect of [Derrida's] many analyses of representative Western thinkers is to give the impression that traditional philosophical discourse is monolithically preoccupied with a formally self-sufficient set of logocentric issues. . . ." Notice the tentative formulations: "the effect of," "give the impression that"; the problem is that such effects and impressions are logocentric readings of logocentrism, whereas Derrida's readings are not simply logocentric and may indeed be marked, as Lentricchia concedes, by specific "historical colorations" (p. 189).

[38]"Decentering cannot be a philosophic or scientific act as such. . . . It was normal that the breakthrough was more secure and more penetrating on the side of literature and poetic writing" (*Of Grammatology*, p. 92).

position while reconstructing its sublimating or idealizing genealogy, and the irruptive emergence of a new 'concept,' a concept which no longer allows itself, never allowed itself to be understood in the previous régime."[39] Such an activity might be negotiated in a number of ways, but what marks the usual Derridean project is its constant warnings that we must be "careful," "rigorous," "vigilant," moving by "perilous necessity," avoiding "regressions" into the "naive concepts" or "uncritical oppositions" being deconstructed or, inversely, too easy an escape to a place mistakenly "outside the classical oppositions."[40]

The deconstructions in "literature," by contrast, are never as explicitly constrained by warnings against wandering into areas under deconstruction; instead they slide and fluctuate, veering eccentrically between moments of centering and decentering. This instability is part of a continuing challenge to all sorts of rigor, since the requirements of rigor may (though they need not) result in all too easy a dismissal of apparently conventional tactics. Such indeed seems to be Paul de Man's worry when, having affirmed that literature "is the only form of language free from the fallacy of unmediated expression," he dissents from one of Derrida's readings: "If . . . Rousseau escapes from the logocentric fallacy precisely to the extent that his language is literary, then . . . the myth of the priority of oral language over written language has always already been demystified by literature."[41] This hardly need be taken, however, as a blanket characterization of literature as deconstructed,[42] and we need not be

---

[39]*Positions, Diacritics* 2, no. 4 (1972):36.
[40]*La dissémination*, p. 11; *Of Grammatology*, pp. 61, 74, 75, 82.
[41]*Blindness and Insight*, pp. 17, 138.
[42]On de Man's reading, "Rousseau's theory of representation is not directed toward meaning as presence and plenitude but toward meaning as void" (*Blindness and Insight*, p. 127); yet meaning as "void" is present to consciousness or functions as presence, and the substitution of "void" for "presence" (or of temporality for synchrony; *ibid.*, pp. 128–33) comes suspiciously close to negative theology. As to whether literary language "escapes

confined by the alternatives just suggested—on the one hand, that owing to the fictive status of the literary sign, all literature is "always already" demystified and, on the other hand, that deconstruction mostly or best takes place in post-Nietzschean writing. At issue in many texts is a troping that works undecidably both with and against logocentric strategies.

This has, of course, to some extent been noticed: Derrida describes literary play as a series of complex mediations in and against the concepts of "literature" and of cosmic Book.[43] Literature as *"l'au delà du tout* [the beyond of everything]" is the inscription of a *tout* needing to be supplemented, thereby "opening up the *'jeu littéraire* [literary game or play]' in which 'literature' disappears, along with the figure of the author."[44] Notice that the disappearance, however, is always equivocal or incomplete; it is in a sense rhetorical even as it questions rhetoric: dissemination "marks the common . . . limits of rhetoric, formalism, and thematism, as of the system of their exchange."[45] Dissemination, or what I here call "rhetoricity," may be construed as a useless doubleness frequently obfuscated by narrative structures and readers' expectations of beginning-middle-end sequences or of some version of the classical determinations of plot, character, and theme.

Within those determinations, the supposedly distinct in-

---

from the logocentric fallacy," this can seem to be reversed even as it seems to be reiterated: "the deconstruction of metaphysics, or 'philosophy,' is an impossibility to the precise extent that it is 'literary'" (*Allegories of Reading*, p. 131). "Demystification," however, is not "deconstruction," since the former claims to come up with some reductive truth, however unsavory, while the latter makes no such claim. What is worth noticing here is the way that "literature" is allied with "rhetoric" in the specific sense of being located in the gap between trope and persuasion, so that "the critique of metaphysics is structured as an aporia between performative and constative utterance" (*ibid*), and can never finally be accomplished.

[43]*La dissémination*, p. 54.
[44]*Ibid*., p. 64.
[45]*Ibid*., p. 42.

terests of morals, rhetoric, and poetry may intrude as threats into one another's proper realms; such certainly seems to be the age-old issue in Wayne Booth's *The Rhetoric of Fiction*: "My subject is the technique of non-didactic fiction. . . . Is there any defense that can be offered, on aesthetic grounds, for an art full of rhetorical appeals?"[46] Moving within the oppositions didactic/nondidactic and aesthetic/rhetorical, Booth undertakes "to free both novelists and readers from the constraints of abstract rules about what novelists must do," yet he ends by warning, didactically enough, against the "morality of impersonal narration."[47] Even classical rhetoric, however, is not so easily to be positioned for or against "morality" or "aesthetic grounds," since it seemed uncannily to evade such classification. Though its basics are named tropes, rhetoric often held power in unnamed and potentially dangerous interstices between selves and community.

The rhetoricity, indeed, of self-questioning narratives starts in an often vertiginous task of bridging or aiming, a task that involves an otherness in self-presence: I am distinct from my past, which is other than me now; I am aware of and distinct from the other with whom I communicate. Although an attention to otherness may already be an effort to lessen it, where Husserl speaks of "modification" and of "harmonious syntheses,"[48] the narrator in (say) Augustine, Cervantes, or Proust will find the effort to confront otherness or to transcend its transcendence to be tinged almost unavoidably with delusion. The delusion is especially noticed in self-questioning texts, which call attention to the literary effort as speech act and thus to the cleft that necessarily divides, as Derrida remarks, the singularity of any speech act, just as it does a signature as event (since to function as iden-

[46]*The Rhetoric of Fiction* (Chicago: University of Chicago Press, 1961), preface, n.p.

[47]*Ibid.*, pp. 377–98.

[48]*Cartesian Meditations*, trans. D. Cairns (The Hague: Nijhoff, 1960), p. 115.

tification, signatures must be unique, but also more than one).[49] The cleft can be concealed if ruptures or lacks are tacitly filled in, but they must be less concealed in texts, such as those which will interest us, where rhetorical need is heightened as speech acts turn out to be vulnerable.

In traditional or "readerly" narratives,[50] there is a certain containment or disguising of vulnerabilities; sequence and progression make sense in socially common perceptions that in effect mediate oppositions. "Authority" may be one crucial indicator of such mediations, and it inevitably involves, as the Frankfurt school has insisted, social and familial dimensions that my stress in this book on the Cartesian gesture must perforce minimize.[51] One might nonetheless notice a movement from the relatively isolated Cogito in the texts of Augustine, Descartes, and Cervantes to the ostensibly fuller contexts in those of Sterne and Faulkner. What seems to happen is that the Cogito in the very act of making a family or of claiming a genealogy also undoes their very possibility: kinship becomes one more element in its self-(un-)doing.

III

It would be all too easy to link the fate of the family, or of the self, with the fate of authority. Writers of self-questioning narratives have usually avoided doing so. Their tactics are nonetheless enmeshed in the web of metaphysics: they struggle against anonymity (or the utter minimum of authority), noting their efforts, traditionally enough, as an engendering or a fabricating, as a genealogy or a machine.

[49]"Signature Event Context," trans. S. Weber and J. Mehlman, in *Glyph 1* (Baltimore: Johns Hopkins University Press, 1977), p. 192.

[50]On "readerly" narratives, see Roland Barthes, *S/Z*, trans. R. Miller (New York: Hill & Wang, 1974).

[51]On Max Horkheimer's and Theodor Adorno's rejections of dualism, see Martin Jay, *The Dialectical Imagination: A History of the Frankfurt School and the Institute of Social Research, 1923–1950* (Boston: Little, Brown, 1973), pp. 46–47, 61, 118–19.

The Rhetoric of Doubtful Authority

Narratives of genealogy are mythic and communal, plotted to accord with marriages and family sequences; they include theogonies, catalogs, and family traditions spanning several generations, as in Hesiod, Balzac, Mann, or Faulkner. Narratives of fabrication or machinery, which may be marked as Cartesian, are of the solitary, introspective, rationally calculating self-making self; here Robinson Crusoe, Don Quixote, Walter Shandy, or Faulkner's Sutpen might be mentioned. Genealogical and mechanical metaphors are often confusingly intertwined, but still it can be said that the Cartesian mode gains in strength: the novel's history (according to Edward W. Said) shows an "increasing awareness of a gap between the representations of fictional narrative and the fruitful, generative principle of human life."[52] Temporality becomes nongenerational or nothing (so St. Augustine sensed) but distensibility.

The very rift between generative and mental sequences is made into a beginning point for self-questioning structures. Cervantes, for instance, takes a position difficult to place; if his narrative seems as "organic" as it seems "conceptual,"[53] any such apparent equation is itself ironized. This can be tied to questions of authority: self-questioning texts like the *Confessions* or *Don Quixote* are without an authorizing father, or the self is unidentifiable by lineage. They are often attributed to orphans: the *Discourse on Method* and *Lazarillo de Tormes*, for instance, are doubly abandoned: the protagonists have no presiding parents and the authors, in not naming themselves, offer detached texts. This is distrustful, but depicted motivations for doubt are compelling in both instances. Once Lazarillo's head is bashed against an iron bull,

---

[52]*Beginnings*, p. 146. Said's thesis is extended in Patricia Tobin, *Time and the Novel: The Genealogical Imperative* (Princeton: Princeton University Press, 1978).

[53]On "organic" and "conceptual," see Georg Lukács, *Theorie des Romans* (Berlin: P. Cassirer, 1920), p. 74.

he urges himself to stay always awake—an exigent version of Cartesian lucidity. Fearing hunger, he makes mechanically repeated counts of all scraps of food, as Descartes makes "enumerations" of mental links. Both narrators hope that their narratives will merit them the shelter of someone's home or at least a gain in respectability; they thus seem rhetorically calculating. We will find this, moreover, again and again. *Don Quixote* and *Tristram Shandy* show engaging machines, knightly in Don Quixote's case, militant or argumentative in Uncle Toby's and Walter's. Machinery involves plotting, devising, scheming, machinations. As against art in general, self-questioning art seems artful—machinery bearing a somewhat counterfeit relation to inspiration, as if a self were trying to endow itself with what the Muses would not.

In this book I shall be concerned with such efforts or, to recapitulate, with what might be called the Cartesian gesture as inscribed in texts that need not be typed as philosophical or literary, for if the former type is said to labor under an illusion of having mastered or authorized its tropes, the latter may share that illusion with only slight variations. I suggest here a few cross-cutting moments of "authority" as doubtful or self-questioning, and the subtitle is intended to indicate a collection of strategies rather than a survey of types or, still less, a quest in the style of Ernst R. Curtius or Erich Auerbach to re-suture a broken humanistic tradition.[54] I remark instead a number of tactics, stressing at all points that if they involve the "rhetoric," "psychology," and "history" of self-questioning narratives, they do so only in a certain sense, since precisely such terms are under interrogation. My effort

[54]See Ernst R. Curtius, *European Literature and the Latin Middle Ages*, trans. W. Trask (New York: Harper & Row, 1963), p. viii; Erich Auerbach, *Literary Language and Its Public in Late Latin Antiquity and in the Middle Ages*, trans. R. Manheim (New York: Pantheon, 1965), p. 6. For histories and typologies, see for instance Robert Alter, *Partial Magic: The Novel as a Self-Conscious Genre* (Berkeley: University of California Press, 1975); R. W. B. Lewis, *The Picaresque Saint* (Philadelphia: Lippincott, 1959); Steven Kellman, *The Self-Begetting Novel* (New York: Columbia University Press, 1980).

The Rhetoric of Doubtful Authority

can be considered deconstructive to the extent that it implicitly questions the Cartesian questioning, not only by remarking a text's inconsistencies in rhetorical strategy but also by
situating moments of doubtfulness or nondecision, or on the
contrary (as one commentator puts it), of "certain very precise *ethico-theoretical decisions.*"[55]

IV

Here might be raised again the question of authority and
its questioning, this time in relation to what the following
readings may or may not implicitly challenge. As almost everyone knows, the Anglo-American scene in literary studies
has lately been agitated by sharp divisions between critics influenced by Continental, particularly French, developments
and by critics dubious of foreign things and eager to carry
on with business as usual. Although the latter critics feel
threatened by the Continental influx, the resistance they put
up is almost invariably infirm, since they revert uncritically
to precisely the concepts being challenged.[56] It is unlikely,

[55]Rodolphe Gasché, "Deconstruction as Criticism," *Glyph 6* (Baltimore:
Johns Hopkins University Press, 1979), p. 190; Gasché's emphasis.
[56]For accounts of the effects of Continental theorizing, see Geoffrey
Hartman, "Literary Criticism and Its Discontents," *Critical Inquiry* 30 (1976):
203–20; Frank Lentricchia, *After the New Criticism*, pp. 156–210; "Unquiet
Flow the Dons," *Newsweek* 97 (February 16, 1981):95–96. For a specific controversy, see J. Hillis Miller, "Tradition and Difference," *Diacritics* 2, no. 4
(1972):6–13, and M. H. Abrams, "The Deconstructive Angel," *Critical Inquiry* 3 (1977):425–38 (also "Rationality and Imagination in Cultural History," *Critical Inquiry* 2 [1976]: 455–58). Abrams tries to argue for governing
norms by which to establish a text's "central core" of meanings, but he, like
others, charges the poststructuralists with clinging to distinctions that actually they question: he believes that Derrida can be faulted for privileging
écriture, but delimits the term (*ibid.*, p. 428) in ways that Derrida repeatedly
warns against. Similarly Hazard Adams reproaches the poststructuralists for
a simplistic signifier/signified dualism, and Hayden White accuses Derrida
of treating the *langue/parole* and metaphor/metonymy distinctions as "the
fundamental categories of Being" (*Directions for Criticism*, ed. M. Krieger and
L. S. Dembo [Madison: University of Wisconsin Press, 1977], pp. 60–83,
107). Such comments not only are misinformed but suggest desperation;
the commentators are left, as they sometimes recognize, without recourse.
In *Literature against Itself* (Chicago: University of Chicago Press, 1979),

moreover, that poststructuralist developments can easily be dismissed, for fashionable though the developments may be, they affect the key assumptions of history and criticism; "the question of the sign," writes Derrida, "is itself more or less, or in any event something other, than a sign of the times."[57]

Poststructuralist readings, especially Derrida's, may nonetheless be somewhat too timely, I have contended, since they are relatively seldom of the more or less classic narratives to be considered here. More is at stake, however, than adding yet more readings, this time decentering ones, to those which already exist; more is at stake, since decentering readings implicitly question the process of reading itself as a transmitting of humanistic themes. While the critics who elaborate such themes usually believe themselves to be the last *auctores* to conserve communal values, they are often reticent about the ways in which their allegiances may be tied to the mechanisms of entrenched social and cultural power. No doubt to some extent on account of institutionally motivated anxiety and ignorance, they aggressively pose questions about what deconstruction is, about whether it has bearings on literature, and if so, just what sorts of messages it might come up with. Although the questions themselves are questionable, the following readings may move readers (though an introduction can make no promises) in the direction of showing the questions' insufficiencies. Since the readings largely constitute what is known as practical criticism, they may pander to what William James called "the cash value of an idea": they are focused on well-known texts (and often on their best-known passages) by way of foregrounding, at

---

Gerald Graff is concerned to resist critical theory that "weakens the educational claims of literature and leaves the literature teacher without a rationale for what he professes" (p. 7). Although he objects to suggestions by poststructuralists that the questioning of mimesis is by now well known (pp. 5, 19, 157), the problem seems to be mostly Graff's, since he offers no consideration whatsoever of Derrida's *La dissémination* or of any text by Foucault.

[57]*Writing and Difference*, trans. A. Bass (Chicago: University of Chicago Press, 1978), p. 3.

times, a deconstructionist perspective. The foregrounding occurs only at times, however, since the readings are of doubtful authority (there can be no "pure" deconstruction) and are offered only as possible readings among others.

With regard to the authority of institutional power, deconstructionist radicality, which puts Hegelian and Marxian dialectic into question, must assume some as yet unknown guises. Such a situation may provoke understandable impatience; Edward W. Said, for instance, believes that Jacques Derrida and even Michel Foucault are politically not radical enough. Although he esteems their ways of contesting the "self-confirming operations of culture," including literary criticism, he is discontent with the limitations particularly of Derrida's endeavor: "On the one hand there is Derrida's vigilance in exposing . . . small mistakes . . . , on the other, there is Derrida appealing to the influence of a philosophy of presence. . . . Yet the mediating agency between the level of detail and the superstructural level is neither referred to nor taken into account."[58] The attitude here is couched (purposely?) in terms that would be suspect from a Derridean perspective: "small mistakes," "mediating agency," "superstructural," "referred to," and of course "Derrida." This is not necessarily to point to irreconcilable divergences or to disparage Said's exasperation with Foucault's "curiously passive" attitude toward praxis or with Derrida's inability "to get hold of the local material density and power of ideas as historical actuality."[59] It is, however, to suggest that judgments about the apparent scope of deconstruction may quickly lead to a discourse with all too familiar contours, and that the

[58]"The Problem of Textuality: Two Exemplary Positions," *Critical Inquiry* 4 (1978):681, 679.

[59]*Ibid.*, pp. 710, 701. Interestingly, in *Orientalism* (New York: Pantheon, 1978), Said delimits his analysis at a very definite point: he discusses the Middle East neither apart from a certain kind of discourse nor in its discourse about itself. See Michael Beard, "Between West and World," *Diacritics* 9, no. 4 [1979]:2–12.

Questioning the Question of Authority

Derridean dislocation may be powerful precisely to the extent of its unpredictability, its strangeness, and above all, its slowness.

Such characteristics might be called monstrous, were it not that "monsters" as frequently map as subvert an economy of mimetic doubling. Monstrosities are traditionally miracles or exceptions that are taken to "prove" the ways of God or the rules of nature;[60] even so, insistent domestication (especially) is makeshift, and the Derridean enterprise in its monstrosity is part of a refusal to espy in the distance some new homeland:

> There is a kind of question, let us still call it historical, whose *conception, formation, gestation,* and *labor* we are only catching a glimpse of today. I say these words with eyes turned [*tournés*], to be sure, toward the operations of childbearing—but also toward those who . . . turn them away [*les détournent*] before the still unnamable that announces itself, and cannot do so . . . except under the species of a nonspecies, in the formless, mute, infant, and terrifying form of monstrosity.[61]

These remarks might be kept in mind in the pages to follow, where the question of authority, apparently limited by classic texts, becomes marginally human, bringing doubles, changelings, homunculi, orphans, half-breeds, bastards, and non-faces. Although this study, a loosely sewn bundle, may prove more useful in a delivery than the Shandean Dr. Slop's knotted green bag, it may or may not help to extract some as yet unheard-of praxis.

[60]See Jean Céard, *La nature et les prodiges* (Geneva: Droz, 1977), and John B. Friedman, *The Monstrous Races in Medieval Art and Thought* (Cambridge: Harvard University Press, 1981). On monstrous doubling, see René Girard, *Violence and the Sacred,* trans. Patrick Gregory (Baltimore: Johns Hopkins University Press, 1977), esp. pp. 143–68.

[61]*L'écriture et la différence* (Paris: Seuil, 1967), p. 428; Derrida's emphasis. On monstrosity, see also *Of Grammatology,* pp. 5, 38, 41, 42; *La carte postale* (Paris: Flammarion, 1980), p. 189; *Glas* (Paris: Galilée, 1974), pp. 26, 87, 106, 197; *La vérité en peinture* (Paris: Flammarion, 1978), pp. 143, 164.

2

Doubling-Making
St. Augustine's *Confessions*

> I asked the whole fabric of the world about my God, and
> it answered me, "I am not he, but he has made me [*non ego
> sum, sed ipse me fecit*]."
> —*Confessions*

The God of Genesis speaks at least twice, once when
he creates the world and then when he warns Adam and Eve
about the tree. Whether or not these be two discrete kinds of
speaking, the second fails spectacularly, possibly because the
serpent as God's "subtle" opponent offers to account for the
taboo on knowledge whereas God had simply said, obey it
"lest you die" (Gen. 3:1–6).[1] Having lost rhetorically to the
serpent, God implements the fall by cursing and shatters the
tower of Babel. There would be new conditions for speech,
and reading would necessarily be complex, for now men,
too, would be "subtle."

If humans are free yet fallen, they may misunderstand (in
their subtlety) the very language that might lead them toward God. This means that even—or especially—divine language might fail, and indeed God almost invariably speaks
through signs, while his prophetic spokesmen are reluctant
or troubled. Moses worries that the people "will not believe
me or listen to my voice," and though God promises to "be
with your mouth" and provides terrible plagues, he for a

[1]References are to the Revised Standard Version.

44

long time cannot convince Pharaoh to release the He-
brews—a situation only obscurely explained by saying that
God "hardened Pharaoh's heart" (Exod. 4:1–21, 10:27).
Later, Jeremiah—like other prophets—would be concerned
at the unresponsiveness of his contemporaries; predictions
had to be inscribed for future generations, and eventually a
tradition of typologies would show that prophecies were being—or had been, or would shortly be—"fulfilled." The
New Testament, just so, defines itself as a figural enrich-
ment of the Old, and Jesus' hermeneutic skills set him off
from—and against—his opponents ("all who heard him
were amazed," and he resists Satan's scriptural citations)
(Luke 2:46–47, 4:1–13). His reading is active in that the law
and prophets are to be interpreted more exigently than before, but passive in that he follows what has been pre-
scripted, refusing to deviate: "the Son of man goes as it has
been determined" or "as it is written of him" (Luke 22:22,
Matt. 26:24). A mutual reinforcement joins specific events
and prophetic texts into an "identity" of self: the Hebrew
people are "the same" through time, and so is their Messiah:
Jesus acts as the texts say, so he "must" be the figure they
describe.[2]

If this seems suspect, the narrative urges, through Jesus,
that conventional cognition be transformed: "you know how
to interpret the appearance of earth and sky; but why do
you not know how to interpret the present time?" (Luke
12:56). Various readings of "the present time" accord with
a story in which Jesus' authority is increasingly rejected until
with the resurrection it "must" be read as a troping (inversion or transposition) of worldly power: his kingdom can

[2]Commentators have suggested, with varying degrees of assertiveness,
that Jesus may have calculated and provoked what happened to him: see
James Barr, *Old and New in Interpretation* (New York: Harper & Row, 1966),
p. 138; Sir Edwyn Hoskyns and Noel Davey, *The Riddle of the New Testament*
(1931; repr. London: Faber, 1968), p. 175; Hugh Schonfield, *The Passover
Plot* (1965; repr. New York: Bantam, 1971).

only be heavenly. Although judgment day will be an annulment of profane temporality, the Gospel texts mention rather than narratively incorporate that day, placing it in an indefinite future as an event that is unexpected yet inevitable. They thus draw rhetorically on the authority not only of narrative but of its potential negation. The conflicting implications are of a promised final verdict and of temporal openness toward God's incomplete self-disclosure: "Now we see in a mirror dimly, but then face to face. Now I know in part; then I shall understand fully, even as I have been fully understood" (1 Cor. 13:12).

I

Augustine's *Confessions*, which turns on such partial disclosures and in which autobiographical narrative is negated after book 9, continually cites biblical texts of God's mediated "I-thou" communications. Although the Psalms and Epistles are particular favorites, another precedent for the Augustinian confessional plight is the Book of Job, where the protagonist and his comforters loudly protest that each speaks empty words. As Augustine probably noticed, Job, despite contrary appearances, is not structured so that a series of erroneous theological views is replaced by progressively "superior" views. The voice out of the whirlwind does climax the story, but the Lord's words (which hardly differ from those of the human contenders[3]) matter less than that it is he who utters them. Voice is decisive because underlying the problem of accepting God's will is the quite possibly more painful problem of whether communication with him is even possible: "Call and I will answer; or let me speak, and do thou reply to me" (Job 13:22). In the Augustinian text, no such request is answered by a whirlwind appearance; God is seen

[3]Cf. Job 11:7–9, 12:9–23, 26:7–14, 37:15–24.

instead through a mirror dimly—*per speculum in aenigmate.* This should, it seems, merit attention. Although medieval theological or theological-literary texts, such as those of Boethius, for example, or even Dante, are often ignored— presumably as "logocentric"—by poststructuralist critics,[4] the subversion of logocentrism is said "always already" to have started. How is this "always already" to be read, we might ask, in medieval theological instances? How much "free-play" is to be found in Augustine's *Confessions*, and what might be said to happen there to a decentered "self" and to the onto-theological constraints that, with the narrator's conversion, purportedly rectify it? Aspects of the question can be located in the Augustinian problem of "confession" itself, that is, in the tactics—and radical questioning —of the "communication" of the narrator with God, with himself, and with readers. Any apparent metaphysical "resolution" of that problem turns out, rhetorically or psychologically, to be not quite decisive.

Since conversion is crucial to the *Confessions*, I will start there. As some readers may be startled to learn, the episode in which Augustine hears a voice urging him to read (*"Tolle, lege"*) before his conversion may be, in Pierre Courcelle's terms, a "literary fiction" rather than a "historical truth."[5] This would seem peculiar, since "confession" by definition should be strictly truthful and since the direction of the entire Augustinian itinerary, with conversion as its decisive moment, is away from errors and lies. Without entering into discussions as to how far Courcelle is warranted in his

[4]Some relevant exceptions are Eugene Vance, "Augustine's *Confessions* and the Grammar of Selfhood," *Genre* 4 (1973):1–28; Margaret Ferguson, "St. Augustine's Region of Unlikeness: The Crossing of Exile and Language," *Georgia Review* 29 (1975):842–64. See also Marcia Colish, "St. Augustine's Rhetoric of Silence Revisited," *Augustinian Studies* 9 (1978):15–24; Kenneth Burke, *The Rhetoric of Religion* (Berkeley: University of California Press, 1970).

[5]*Recherches sur les Confessions de S. Augustin* (Paris: Boccard, 1968), pp. 188–202.

The Rhetoric of Doubtful Authority

claims, one might speculate on the strong possibility that Augustine would have regarded such an embellishment not as a lapse from truth but on the contrary as truth's intensification. By the rhetorical theory of the *De Doctrina Christiana*, the "slavery" and "death" of the soul are to be confined to literal meanings,[6] and in the *Confessions*, having disclosed the power of allegorical reading for his conversion, Augustine would be likely to use allegory to show his own figural rebirth.

This is hardly to qualify the contention that the notion of "confession" is problematic; it is, but not owing to questions of empirical referentiality. The problem comes with assertions that Christian figurative language is somehow less erroneous or sinful than the language of secular rhetoric. Connected with this problem, and vital to his story's suspense, is whether Augustine, converted, will know God, and if so, how he will communicate that knowledge. The second question is pertinent, since with conversion Augustine relinquishes a career as secular rhetorician and presumably employs thereafter a "better"—Christian and allegorical—rhetoric to convey what he has learned. An autobiographical narrative, however, and much else besides, may be tied too closely to temporality and to a supposedly abandoned rhetoric for the author properly to represent the "higher" stages of his journey. Indeed the very notion of temporal representation is considered flimsy in book 11, and no doubt Augustine's divided attitude (amazed yet disappointed) toward his discovery of time as the *distentio animae* (11.26.33)[7] has something to do with his narrative's doubled perspective and his

[6]*On Christian Doctrine*, trans. D. W. Robertson, Jr. (New York: Bobbs-Merrill, 1958), book 3.V.9, p. 84; Latin citations are from the *Corpus Christianorum*, Series Latina, v. 32 (Turnholti: Pontifici, 1962).

[7]References are by book, chapter, and section to *The Confessions*, trans. John K. Ryan (Garden City: Doubleday, 1960); the Latin is from the bilingual edition of Pierre de Labriolle (Paris: Société d'Edition "Les Belles Lettres," 1944).

attempted erasure of "external" autobiographical narrative (after book 9).

In the difficult search of book 11, Augustine is troubled that "time" seems to crumble before his cognitive gaze. He observes that time can be measured by a psalm-reciting voice but also that the time so marked has no "what" except in the mind, which conjoins syllables in a fragile *distentio* of itself. The capacity for *distentio* (memory-intuition-anticipation), which at first glance had seemed a marvel, also spreads out and flattens the soul; it differs-defers. It bears a makeshift resemblance to logocentric eternity and a strong resemblance, Augustine suggests, to the erroneousness familiar from his earlier sinful ways (11.29.39). In relation to God's Word, the voice whose syllables arrive and pass away must be "distantly other" (11.6.8). How then is that Word to be approached, heard, known, confessed?

The question is reiterated at every turn. The starting narrator, for example, performs a speech act that is immediately shadowed by doubts. His *"Magnus es, domine,"* however familiar as liturgical convention, is posed as a dilemma (and so in effect interrogated as a convention) for a narrator who asks, "grant me to know and understand which is first, to call upon you or to praise you, and also which is first, to know you or to call upon you?" (1.1.1). Should not the opening sentence have already quieted and answered the query? Had that opening sentence somehow been neither praise nor knowledge nor calling? To wonder about priorities in the give-and-take of exchange is to wonder about what kind of transaction—if any—can have occurred: "You pay debts, although you owe no man anything; you cancel debts, and lose nothing" (1.4.4). Such an economics is none; it simply repeats the question, Can the exchanges between humans find any "true" analogy to supposed or desired exchanges with God? Is the "thou" of God in relation to human selves metaphoric or metonymic or neither? ("In truth, are you anything at all, that I may speak to you?"; 2.6.12). The long series of opening questions "about" or "to" God is rhetorically forceful because the questions are also—piercingly perhaps because only—about, or to, the asking self: "Is there anything in me that can contain you?" (1.2.2). This question, with its two poles, is part of a doubleness in the *Confessions* of paired terms (time/eternity, flesh/spirit), which fail to satisfy the narrator even in the most versatile oscillations (as opposites, supplements, repetitions, analogues).

II

The pairings or doublings allow, however, for certain strategies of narrative rhetoric. The "now" of performative utterances regarding God must be "present" for any reader any time as "this" instance of action. The event always happens even though, for the same reason, it *has already* happened. The doubleness is not quite symmetrical with another doubleness, that of the narrator-narrating and the narrator-narrated. With his conversion as *the* allegedly unifying turn among other, allegedly dispersive, turns (tropes), the narrator can paradoxically "divide" himself into pre- and postconversion identities: he emphatically is both "different from" and "the same as" himself, and this is complicitous with a strong pressure to privilege the conversion as a hiatus.[8] The narrator shows his earlier "self" as sinfully errant and his confessing, present "self" correctively above, witnessing the first (happily aware of God's once "secret" providential script; 1.12.19, 4.14.22, 5.7.13, 5.8.15). Yet there is also a counterpressure to admit that "the same I" is involved, since the point of confession is to establish by an enlightened opposite (grace or knowledge) that the earlier doings can

[8]On this and related aspects, see Robert Jordan, "Time and Contingency in St. Augustine," in R. A. Markus, ed., *Augustine* (Garden City: Doubleday, 1972), pp. 255–79.

properly be called sinful. Although in this, too, the postconversion narrator undeniably assumes himself on—or nearer to—"God's side," his more godly self strangely reduplicates the earlier, supposedly superseded errings and questings in the performative "now" of worry, questioning, and beseeching. The conversion, we recall, has several related aspects: (1) hearing Ambrose's allegorical readings of Scripture and (2) Ponticianus's story followed by the "*Tolle, lege*" voice, leading to (3) a reading of Romans 13 and (4) a decision to reject sexual activity as well as (5) the teaching of secular rhetoric. The young orator, "proud of neck," "committed fornication against you" by speaking to applause (1.13.21, 3.3.5); his conversion, by comparison, is to be a self-effacing submission of voice and will.

The submission of voice begins when the as yet unconverted Augustine, having no interest in Ambrose's subject (*res*), tries to listen only to the figures and eloquence (*verba*). Such listening proves impossible: "with the words, which I loved, there entered into my mind the things themselves [*res etiam*]" (5.14.24). What sort of *res*, however, is this? In the *De Doctrina Christiana*, the *res* is meticulously separated from the *signum*: "Strictly speaking [*proprie*], I have here called a 'thing' that which is not used to signify something else, like wood, stone, cattle, and so on."[9] Even on the assumption (which Augustine entertains elsewhere) that there are "mental things," the rhetorical tactics here seem suspect: precisely at the moment Augustine claims that "things" enter him, he makes clear that they are *not* things but signs. That the signs in this instance have both "literal" and "spiritual" dimensions in no way differentiates them from other signs, except for some untold "special" quality of their spirituality, a quality conveyed by the very term for what (in itself or in a sign) is *not* semiotic or spiritual but corporeal or dumb. The narra-

[9]*On Christian Doctrine*, 1.II.2, p. 8.

tor thus tropes what "strictly speaking" (if it is to remain the *res etiam*) he urges—morally and eschatologically—should not be troped.[10] He inverts or allegorizes what by his own definition is only a part—the "lower" part—of the allegorical sign. In the rhetorical (and sexual) operation here, a listening Augustine is pierced and affected by "direct" doctrine, and the mediation of sign is apparently—or apparently allegorically—bypassed. Supposedly Ambrose "would draw aside the veil" (6.4.6). But as we shall notice further, the veil—of mystery, dissimulation, modesty—can be opened only upon others: what is drawn aside is both from and of literal meanings, disclosing (despite contrary suggestions) not the silent simplicity of things but other aspects of allegorical double-talk.

The unveiling/veiling marks, here and elsewhere, the force of desire. The *De Doctrina Christiana* urges not only that "things" and "signs" be conscientiously kept apart but that natural and conventional signs be carefully distinguished. Natural signs, such as involuntary facial expressions, "make us aware of something . . . without [there having been] any will to signify," whereas conventional signs "are those which living creatures show to one another for the purpose of conveying, in so far as they are able, the motion of their spirits, or something which they have sensed or understood." Having admitted natural signs as signs, Augustine excludes them from further discussion, claiming that they may not "truly" be signs at all;[11] he moves quickly thus to suppress possible accidents, slippages, or gaps between (or within) agents, messages, intentions, meanings.

Although serious communicative difficulties remain despite this narrowing of the field, Augustine attributes them to divinely purposive obscurity (for aiding our faith) and to mistaken (but rectifiable) readings of Scripture. The stakes

[10]*Ibid.*, 2.I.1, p. 34.
[11]*Ibid.*, 2.I.2–2.II.3, pp. 34–35.

here are eschatological; charity is thus crucial, and allegory restrains "wrong" possibilities even as it vindicates itself. To read literally is the "death of the soul"; it is to take signs only for things and to be enslaved, beastlike, to the flesh. The economy is somberly efficient: scriptural passages not literally pertinent "must be figurative," and "an evil of wandering error [is] to interpret signs in a useless way."[12] The whole hermeneutics, it could be said, of (non-)communication and (mis-)reading is geared into the machinery of salvation—its obstacles, exclusion, and perhaps conversely, its possible "end" in a more direct vision of the Lord.

If reading is especially valued as communicative, reading—even controlled scriptural reading—is no more (and, convention has it, much less) "direct" than seeing or hearing. A number of tactics, however, valorize proper reading and writing by making them mimetic of Scripture; among such tactics are not only citation, allusion, and exegesis but the dramatized effects of scriptural reading. Doublings such as "thing"/text, text/text, and text/effect are themselves repeated or redoubled and are strongly at work in the conversion narrative. Ponticianus tells of two associates, one of whom reads from a biography of Anthony's conversion and is converted, the second associate then imitating the first. An Augustine distressed by his hesitancy to do likewise is urged to read (as was Anthony), reads, converts, and is himself immediately imitated by Alypius. As possible instances of what René Girard calls "mimetic desire,"[13] these doubled conversions may be deceptively reconciliatory. While some of them may—as in Augustine's case—temporarily intensify rather than resolve conflicts, they also invite readerly imitation as a stabilizing, though perhaps less controllable, "end." The narrator's mimesis is agonizing as a threatened erasure of social

[12]*Ibid.*, 3.IX.13, p. 87.
[13]*Violence and the Sacred*, trans. Patrick Gregory (Baltimore: Johns Hopkins University Press, 1977), pp. 143–49.

differences: he can duplicate not his predecessors but only his own wayward, noncommunal self: "You stood me face to face with myself, so that I might see how foul I was, how deformed and defiled, how covered with stains and sores. I looked, and I was filled with horror, but there was no place for me to flee . . . from myself" (8.7.16). The onlooking self, positioned by God, is (like God) piercingly self-seeing and all-seeing, yet *at the same time* foul, deformed, defiled. The polarities that strengthen each other are unstably vertiginous; the double is a monster, the monster duplicates itself.[14] The self "is" at once utterly godlike and utterly monstrous. The sinfully evil self (evil "is" not) needs to be brought back into being; its wills have become radically split into unconnected similars or dissociations: mind uncontrols mind—*Unde hoc monstrum?* (8.9.21).

Granted that the self may be divine and monstrous, however, the Girardian identification of doubling and monstrosity is all too self-confirming.[15] Neither mythic nor genetic monsters need be doubles, and indeed they may be terrifying in just that regard: the Cyclops has one eye, and teratology discovers monsters both with repeated parts and with a lack of parts.[16] This is not to suggest that monstrosity and doubling are not often linked, but that the boundaries between proper and improper doubling are more terrifyingly indeterminate than Girard's theory—or Augustine's narrative—allows. The converting (and, as we shall find, the converted) Augustine, for all his "proper" mimetic activity, is never quite at peace, and his rhetorical tactics are notable: the conversion narrative is on the Christian God's "side," and it *pursues* the narrated narrator: "as [Ponticianus] spoke,

[14]*Ibid.*, p. 160.

[15]*Ibid.* "The double and the monster are one and the same being. The myth, of course, emphasizes only one aspect (usually the monstrous aspect) in order to minimize the other."

[16]*Encyclopaedia Britannica*, 1969 ed., s.v. "monster"; L. C. Dunn, "Genetic Monsters," *Scientific American* 182, no. 6 (1950):16–19.

you, O Lord, turned me back upon myself"; "if I tried to turn my gaze from myself, he still went on with the story" (8.7.16).

III

Augustine's monstrous doubling is ostensibly resolved by a violent cancellation of one of the contending opposites: "I made sacrifice, slaying my old self, and hoping . . . in you" (9.4.10). This supposedly leaves a "single" will. But the problem here is that only at its most aberrant can the self "see" its aberration, and the decision to convert may thus seem suspect. The decision, almost forced upon it by a devoutly relentless act of narration, is somehow "literary" or unreal: "I said some such words, . . . I did not speak in my usual way. My brow, cheeks, eyes, color and tone of voice spoke my state of mind more than the words that I uttered" (8.8.19). This is an allegorical reading (body bespeaks mind) of what neither the narrating nor the narrated narrator can have seen directly: it is speculative, specular, specious: how can he "see" himself except in an imagined-remembered *speculum*? God is similarly seen, however, and the narrative begins to counteract vertiginous doubling with reiterated models of sanctioned doubling: Anthony, the associates, Augustine, Alypius, all read and convert. The imitations are controlled by close and imperative text-self connections: when an undecided Augustine opens the Scriptures at random, the verses—which ordinarily (randomly) are no more or less referential than others—can and therefore must (presumably by will as much as by re-cognition) refer to him. The passage to which he opens (Rom. 13:13–14) urges that wavering oppositions be fixed in their "right" places, that flesh be firmly subordinated to mind and will. The conversion thereupon resonates with familiar movements (old to new, slavery to freedom, crucifixion to resurrection), which are gradually to explicate the sanctioned doubling of man "made in God's image."

The doubling during conversion is not simple, however, but involves substitutions. The much-deferred decision to convert is on the one hand extremely risky, since if Augustine does not properly implement it, he will be returned more irremediably than ever to his tormenting errancy and dispersion. On the other hand (and yet as part of the same logic), what Augustine learns precisely in the process of conversion is how to accomplish a series of problematic substitutions for what, in converting, he renounced. Notice for instance that the figure of Continence, who moves him away from his lustful tendencies, takes the form of an attractive woman stretching out her arms to embrace him (8.11.27). She is of course "only" allegorical, and she is described as "virtuously alluring" with a "chaste dignity" (8.11.27). Just so, however, the Augustinian story articulates a number of predictable (and indeed predicted) signs about the tropings of desire or, more specifically, about the joys and sacrifices of allegorical reading.

The infant in book 1 for instance readily learns words, because they are intertwined with strong desire: he notices the things to which words point, and if he desires those things, he calls out their names. He of course soon recognizes that a thing wanted and named is not necessarily obtained and that far more complex operations, known as rhetoric, will be required, though with no guarantee, even then, of satisfaction. If language moreover is ostensive, how speak of those objects of desire which cannot be pointed to—such as God? Regarding those objects, desire will be repeatedly balked, and even the most articulate rhetoricians may seem as speechless (*in-fans*) as crying infants. There are many sorts of crying, even so, and what the *Confessions* wishes to teach is that the things of God can at least partially be named—by allegory—and that the desire for God can at least partially be appeased. Since with the learning of allegorical reading, Augustine will locate himself closer to his journey's goal, we would do well to review how he recounts that learning.

He bitterly complains, to begin with, about his early education, though he also grants that it had some value: "You . . . turned to my advantage the error of all those who kept me at my studies" (1.12.19). His teachers forced him "to learn by heart I know not how many of Aeneas's wanderings, although forgetful of my own, and to weep over Dido's death . . . when all the while . . . dying to you, O God my life" (1.13.20). From his postconversion perspective, the narrator can read the Virgilian text as an allegory of his former state. Although the text is thus conceded to have a meaning, that text is objectionable not only because Aeneas was pagan and not "real" (and so the young Augustine's feelings were dissipated rather than economized) but because the text was allegorizing Augustine's own state and he failed to see this, since he could only read it literally. That particular failure of reading is, of course, typical: Augustine's entire preconversion life is merely a literal series of incidents to whose allegorical significance—that is, God's secret providence—the young Augustine, we are repeatedly told, was utterly blind.

Notice once again, however, that there is a doubleness of valorization of the literal level that will recur, with strange consequences, allegorically. The literal is on the one hand dead, or death: the preconversion narrator was blind in that he could only see his life in literal terms, and was "literally" drawn into Virgil or, just as erroneously, was "literally" excluded, in his naive readings, from the Bible. On the other hand, however, the only value of his early education is precisely that he learned to read literally: he learned the letters that spelled the name Aeneas; he thus learned signs that in themselves were certain and reliable, as opposed to the misleading meanings ("poetic fables") that could be attached to them (1.13.22). Literal signs, it seems, are not deadly if, but only if, they point toward (and are sanctioned by) appropriate allegorical significances.

Is Christian allegory, then, necessarily appropriate? Recall again the passage about Ambrose interpreting Scripture: "at the same time with the words . . . there also entered into my mind the things themselves" (5.14.24). Christian allegorical reading brings mere signifiers, which in themselves are dead, to life, and it carries us into close proximity with divine signifieds. Ambrose is hindered minimally, if at all, by the opacities of mediation; in his cell, as the monks watch him unnoticed, he reads silently, seeming to avoid even the voice and going straight for the meanings: "When he read, his eyes moved down the pages and his heart sought out their meaning, while his voice and tongue remained silent. . . . After sitting for a long time in silence—who would dare to annoy a man so occupied?—we would go away" (6.3.3). At a time when reading was performed orally, Ambrose's reading in silence was impressive; his possible contact with divine signifieds is moreover presumably to be connected with his abilities to remove the veil of allegory: "he would draw aside the veil of mystery" (6.4.6). This latter statement, however, which refers to Ambrose in his speaking rather than in his silence, is itself allegorical; granted that Augustine no longer reads with his earlier eye ("*non illo ocula*"), he is still, or therefore, not certain of those things "that I could not see" (6.4.6). The opening of the allegorical veil, it seems, far from bringing full knowledge, requires belief—and this somewhat strangely betokens (in ways, that is, that will require further allegorizing) our closeness to divine presence. Allegory will never, we may suspect, reach an end.

This is not, however, immediately apparent, and conversion once recounted, Augustine negates (in book 9) the "external" temporal self's narrative. Although the sometimes troublesome narrator/narrated doubleness is largely abandoned in favor of the self as its own object, the "confession" problem is only intensified: has conversion brought a greater "closeness" to God, and if so, how is this to be told? Recall for instance the famous moment at Ostia with his mother:

> We proceeded step by step through all bodily things up to that heaven whence shine the sun and the moon and the stars down upon the earth. We ascended higher yet by means of inward thought and discourse and admiration of your works, and we came up to our own minds. We transcended them, so that we attained to the region of abundance that never fails. [9.10.24]

This moment turns out, perhaps surprisingly, to be an incomplete vision and thus the hope of something fuller ("When shall this be?"; 9.10.25); how otherwise are we to read the agonizing speech acts that still haunt the discourse and make it so poignant? The narrator has supposedly learned, with conversion, of a doubling that should be identification—"not to will what I willed and to will what you willed" (9.1.1). Can submission, however, be performed without cognitive slippage? Granted that historically narratable erring is "past," there is as much possibility for erring (presumably of a different kind) in the "present" quest of a narrator who struggles to systematize the orderings of memory, speech, and creation. In this quest, encounters of the self with itself, as if of an "I" with a "thou," are bound to be artificial (rhetorically, prosopopoeia); communication of self with self is fictive or substitutive, and a questionable model for attempted contact with the Lord.

Augustine experiments perforce with just such a model, and wonders in books 10 and 11 at veiled or ungraspable ("inner" yet somehow always "outer"; 10.8.15) dimensions of self. On the one hand, he finds himself master of a huge world of memory: "even when I dwell in darkness and silence, I bring forth colors in my memory, [and if I call for sounds,] . . . immediately they are there on the spot"

(10.8.13). Sensed temporal events pass away, but their images (and the "things themselves" of abstract thought) are retained in memory, which thus partakes of a reassuring nontemporality (10.9.16). On the other hand, memory is full of deceptions and unknown recesses, and though its images of things are partially classified (10.8.13), Augustine must consult God's light "as to whether they were, as to what they were, and as to what value they possessed" (10.40.65). The suggestion is that if he can place himself in a stable relation to the doubled but *correctly graded* contents of memory, he may move toward rectification of earlier monstrousness. God's assistance is called for, however, not only because the self regresses (10.30.41, 10.31.47) and is uncontrollably enormous (10.8.15, 10.17.26, 10.40.65) but because the investigation of memory, as of temporality, rapidly becomes self-deconstructive; how is it possible, the narrator asks, to remember *"oblivio"* (forgetfulness)? *Oblivio* may be considered as the image not of an external but of an internal *res*, yet it cannot be present as either one or the other. How, indeed, could *oblivio* inscribe a mark on memory; what mark could be the "sign" of nonpresence? Augustinian logocentrism may make this all the more acute: how did forgetfulness "inscribe [*conscribebat*] its image on memory, since by its very presence [it] wipes away whatever it finds already noted there?" The question is not quite resolvable by mystery or assurance ("in some . . . inexplicable [manner], I am certain [*certus sum*] that I have remembered forgetfulness"; 10.16.25). For it is God who seems to be inscribed as just so doubtful a mark as *oblivio*: he is "in" memory only in the manner of something lost and half-forgotten, and the narrator must, if possible, move "beyond" memory (10.19.28, 10.17.26).

He offers to do so in a reading of Genesis that he hopes will supersede the incomplete testimony not only of memory but of created things. Consider his encounter (to recall our epigraph) with the "outer" world: "I asked the heavens, the sun, the moon, and the stars: . . . 'Tell me of my God! Although you are not he, tell me something of him!' With a mighty voice they cried out, 'He made us!' My question was the gaze I turned on them; the answer was their beauty" (10.6.9). The world is amiable—things have voices and answer questions. The voices, however, are immediately translated into silence or space (gaze, beauty) and the directive (in the next paragraph) to move from outer to inner things will yield, as we noted, equivocal results. What is urged is a promisingly close tie between creature and Creator (made and Maker), and a special significance in the process of creation.

IV

An allegorical reading of creation in Genesis resituates—though perhaps only slightly—the problem of confession. In contrast to human words, God's Word speaks eternally, not one thing then another but "all things . . . once and forever" (11.7.9). He makes the world by speaking, but any analogy to human speaking or making must be firmly rejected (11.5.7). Any similarity of Word to word is misleadingly homonymic, and any correlation is conceptually odd: created things can only be signs of him, while he, neither sign nor thing, is unrepresentable, or visible for now at best, in the recurrent phrase from 1 Corinthians 13, *per speculum in aenigmate*. The *De Trinitate* (succeeding the *Confessions* by a few years) gives Augustine's reading: "What we have tried to do is to gain through this image which is ourselves [*quod nos sumus*] some vision, as through a mirror, of him who made us."[17] The mirror offers not only an alternative to self-seeing monstrosity but a possible transit from creature to

[17]*On the Trinity*, XV, 14 (viii), trans. John Burnaby, in *Augustine: The Later Works* (Philadelphia: Westminster, 1955), p. 141. The Latin is from the *Corpus Christianorum*, Series Latina, v. 50a (Turnholti: Pontifici, 1968).

Creator. Attention might well be directed, then, to the *per speculum in aenigmate* trope, which Augustine glosses as an allegorical doubling, or an allegory of allegory: "As the word 'mirror' was intended to signify an image, so the word 'enigma' was meant to stand for a similitude, but one that is obscure and hard to discern. . . . We may understand the apostle to have expressed the notion of certain similitudes adapted for our understanding of God."[18] "Obscure," he says, yet "adapted": the accommodation points to an oddity, "our not seeing that of which we cannot be without the vision. Can any man *not* see his own thought? And can any man see his own thought . . . by inward vision? Both not seeing and seeing are unimaginable."[19] The enigma ("greater," he allows, than the one he explicates) is that within ourselves we cannot see the seeing-source of even what is clearest and closest.

That enigma is eventually to be lessened, so we are to believe, when we see God "face to face." And as if following such a promise, Augustine's doctrine of signs expands, with sometimes surprising rapidity, to the point of dissolution (in what R. A. Markus designates, although excessively, as a "profound shift in perspective"[20]). Whereas in the *De Doctrina Christiana* signs stand for things, in the *De Trinitate* certain unspoken words can present unmediated meanings: "It is possible . . . to understand the meaning of a word, not only before it is uttered aloud, but even before the images of its uttered sounds are rehearsed in thought."[21] This shifts rather than alleviates the problem of communication and *oblivio*: such special words, despite contrary intimations, are like other words in that they operate as signs of something else: "Any man that can understand this unspoken word,

18*Ibid.*, XV, 16 (ix), p. 143.
19*Ibid.*
20"St. Augustine on Signs," in R. A. Markus, *Augustine*, p. 80.
21*On the Trinity*, XV, 19 (x), p. 145.

can see through this mirror and in this enigma a certain likeness of that Word of which it is written: 'In the beginning was the Word, and the Word was with God, and the Word was God.'"[22] The unspoken word and others perhaps like them, if writable, presumably show a closer similitude than ordinary words to God's creation.

In the *Confessions*, just so, to write about making parallels God's making—not simply mimetically or referentially, since the Word is enigmatic, but allegorically—as an unfolding (clarifying and expanding) of enigma. Augustine's attention to Genesis should by all rights fulfill his speech-act yearnings for full communion; it should in some sense "complete" his quest. For if God's making of the world allegorically "converts" the unformed void (13.4.5), Augustine's early life—as the chaotic void converted—"makes" him. It makes him partly into an allegorist, both because Ambrose's readings prepared for conversion and because a postconversion Augustine can map out creation from the turnings of his life: "our darkness displeased us, and we were converted to you, and light was made" (13.12.13; also 13.4.5, 13.5.6). Such allegory enables a deftness at connections: personal making is related not only to cosmogony but to the emerging Church—the evangelists live allegorically, manifesting creation by working "corporeally . . . amid many waters . . . [to] produce mystical deeds and words" (13.20.28). The waters below signify a restless mankind, and the earth (Christian believers) rises out of the sea as a place of solidity. Words of mystery can then be replaced by exemplary actions, which may in turn be read as fulfilling the commandment to increase and multiply:

> I have known a thing to be signified in many ways by the body [*per corpus*] that is understood in one way by the mind, and a thing to be understood in many ways by the mind that is

[22]*Ibid.*

signified in but one way by the body. Consider sincere love
[*simplex dilectio*] of God and neighbor, see how it is expressed
corporeally in many holy rites, and . . . by innumerable turns
of speech. Thus do the offspring of the waters increase and
multiply. Note this again, whoever you are who read these
words [*adtende iterum quisquis haec legis*]. [13.24.36]

Allegory here again is sanctioned by doubling, that is, by
allegorizing itself. Augustine tells the reader to pay attention: the "same" Word generatively expands to control local
languages and signs. In creation-conversion, mind domi-
nates body: multiple corporeal significations are understood
in "one way" while the mind's "one way" finds multiple corporeal expressions.

Creation is a going out, a proliferation of meanings limited by hierarchical ordering; dissemination or sin (Augustine prays) is recuperable, or convertible "back" to God. Yet
the economy's boundaries are defined by deviations, and the
economy itself is enigmatic. The Augustinian quest would
seem "fulfilled" with the chain conversion-text-self-creation-
cosmos-Church and with the text's approximation, by citation or allegory, to the scriptural "firmament of authority"
(13.15.16). The narrator is nonetheless naggingly aware of
potentially tendentious readers with whom he must plead (in
lengthy hermeneutic musings) that different scriptural readings may be variously true rather than contradictory, that
plurality—if seen charitably—may be plenitude. The request for charity is made along with special (and for that reason, possibly countereffective) claims that Augustine hears
God's voice in his "interior ear" (13.29.44, 12.15.18). Troped
though it may be as God's voice, the act of reading ("I hear
your Scripture saying . . ."; 12.13.16) requires distance. Even
when the narrator imagines the angels to know God not
enigmatically but by face, the metaphor is still—strangely,
perhaps—of reading: "Let . . . your angels praise you, they
who have no need to look up at this firmament, or by read-

ing to know your Word. They always behold your face, and without any syllables of time, they read upon it what your eternal will decrees" (13.15.18). The angels read, yet they do not read; they know without reading, but their knowledge is describable only as mediated, at least to the nonangelic.

And indeed allegory as plenitude never quite ends or recompenses the narrator's opening and continuing perplexities. He reads and inscribes God's text: "with us it is still by faith and not yet by sight," adding—more strongly—that when men see "through your Spirit, you see in them" (13.13.14, 13.31.46). This latter claim is directed to the Manichaeans, who doubted the divine authorship of Scriptures and who thus prompted the young narrator to respond that precisely that authorship was most of all to be believed (6.5.7). Here he offers his concluding attack against them by almost alleging that he sees as God sees ("the answer is made to me"), namely that the world was not made piecemeal or by a hostile intelligence (13.30.45). What he must strenuously insist upon—and we might note that he must do so— is the prestige of authorship, of the Author-authored link, of the voices of created beings (such as himself) saying that they do point, if only that, toward their Maker.

3

Cartesian Striptease

Be sure of it; give me the ocular proof.

—*Othello*

. . . it may happen . . . that I might not even have eyes to
see anything.

—*Meditations*

Author of a *Dioptric*, René Descartes stressed seeing
rightly, or seeing what there is to see. To intensify ocularity,
however, is to intensify an inevitable indirection, for the eye
can never see itself seeing from inside, not even with mirrors
or anatomical dissection. And if "it is the soul that sees,"[1]
what can be gained, except metaphorically, by attention to
eyes, since with physical eyes the soul's seeing can never be
seen? Would not the soul's seeing, too, be invisible directly to
itself? And does the soul's seeing then have a blind spot? Or
if the soul needs no eyes to see (*M* 2), how and what does it
see at all? Such questions are of course crudely literal, but
are they really improper? We are asking for no more than

[1]*La dioptrique*, 6: "c'est l'âme qui voit, et non pas l'oeil." References in the
text are hereafter by the number of the rule, part, or meditation, based on
the texts in *Oeuvres de Descartes*, ed. C. Adam and P. Tannery, 10 vols.
(Paris: Vrin, 1953); French as modernized in Descartes, *Oeuvres et Lettres*,
ed. A. Bridoux (Paris: Gallimard, 1953). The English translation of the *Objections and Replies* is from *Philosophical Works of Descartes*, 2 vols., ed. E. S.
Haldane and G. R. T. Ross (Cambridge: Cambridge University Press,
1962); the other translations are mine. Abbreviations are as follows: *R*: *Rules
for the Direction of the Mind*; *D*: *Discourse on Method*; *M*: *Meditations*; *O*: Objections, *RO*: Replies to Objections, in the *Objections and Replies*. Note that the
Replies in Descartes's text are printed in italics.

some sort of equivalent, after all, for a series of traditional and well-established (thus, one would think, proper) figures.

We are not likely, even so, to receive an answer. Could it be indeed that our eyes—or the soul—in the very act of seeing vigilantly may see improperly, that is, not just see poorly, but see what they should not see? What is the soul's role, as Othello in the epigraph might have done well to wonder, in what the eyes see? If thinking they see the unspeakable, how should eyes tell of what they have seen, or is seeing itself a noting, a remarking, and so already a telling?

Such questions appear, sometimes in disguise, on the Cartesian horizon and are entwined with problems of authorial self. The locus of seeing, as of writing, is the "I"; as the English homonymy would have it, an *I* is an *eye*. If so, our questions about seeing might be asked about writing and figuring. Note for instance that just as with the Cogito the eye (or I) of the soul would be linked nondeceptively with its object and with the seeings of different seers (or readers) of the *Meditations*, so the authorial mind, pen, and paper would be linked directly in the act of writing. In his writing as in his Cogito, the Cartesian narrator, who apparently would like to persuade us that he is not a mere figment, engages himself in a driving out of the sign as figure: "If I move one end of a stick, . . . I easily understand that the power by which that part of the stick is moved necessarily also moves, in one and the same instant, all its other parts, because the power is communicated nakedly [*nuda*] rather than existing in some body that carries it [*a quo deferatur*]" (R 9). This is the naked truth: any figure is literally the pen's writing motion:

> The figure received [in perception] is immediately transported to another part of the body, . . . just as now while I write, I understand that at the very moment when each of the characters is set down on the paper, not only is the lower part of the pen moved, but no motion, not even the smallest, can occur in it that does not simultaneously occur in the whole pen; and all

these diverse motions are traced by the upper end of the pen
in the air . . . without anything real being transmitted from one
end to the other. [*R* 12]

The figure here is a perceiving-thinking-moving-writing;
there thus appears to be no loss in transference or communication. The appearance, however, may be deceptive, as when
Jean-Luc Nancy plays the Cartesian clerk: "I desire an illu-
minating, blinding writing. I desire to write with light."[2] Desire is lack; instead of writing with light, the mind and eyes
are only written upon by light. Might not writing be to being
written, even so, as figuring is to figure? "Nothing falls under the senses more easily than figure: it is touched and seen
[*tangitur enim et videtur*]. Nothing false comes of this supposi-
tion" (*R* 12). Passivity brings correctness: our senses "perceive properly speaking in virtue of passivity alone, just as
wax receives a figure from a seal" (*R* 12). Power is in the ma-
teriality of figure and in its utter connectedness with agency.
What happens from text to text, though, to the wax—
and thus the figure? If in the *Regulae* the wax is as accurately
imprinted as are the eyes in seeing (and "this is not asserted
by analogy"; *R* 12), the wax in the *Meditations* will show that
the eyes that deceive us cannot see, but only the mind (*M* 2).
Where the sign (in the *Regulae*) is so close to the referent
that no meaning is lost, the referent (in the first two meditations) is so deceptive that it must be put out of play. What
occurs between the two texts is this putting out of play of
physical seeing—a distancing perforce because of distance.
This brings a heightened pressure of and against rhetorical
figure, for the figure now marks not the identity of vehicle
and meaning, but (as linguistic ideality) the distance between
them.

[2]*Ego Sum* (Paris: Flammarion, 1979), p. 49.

Cartesian Striptease

I

Let us approach the situation obliquely: if the "essence" of the narrator's piece of wax in the *Meditations* not only is known by the mind but is like the mind, can we similarly know the "essence" of the narrator?

Readers have become accustomed to think of Descartes reductively as the *res cogitans* or perhaps the *philosophe au masque*. But there is a point early in the *Meditations* where to all appearances he reveals himself in a situation that is purposely ordinary—so ordinary, indeed, that he and we "cannot reasonably doubt" that this is he: "I am here, seated by the fire, wearing a dressing gown, with this paper in my hands, and other such things" (*M* 1). We presumably visit him in his home, where he is at leisure, dressed in his robe, and possibly ready to go, fairly soon, to bed. The relaxed author is simply "being himself" and is telling us his thoughts.

His leisurely self-disclosure is not, however, entirely innocent: his talk moves to night, dreams, insanity, and nakedness. We noted "naked power" in the *Regulae*, and here the narrator tells us that he is quite unlike the insane, who would deny their human corporeality or believe themselves to be "dressed in gold and purple when they are totally naked [*tout nus*]" (*M* 1). He separates himself from them but also claims a certain affinity:[3] "how many times have I happened to dream at night that I was in this place, by the fire, dressed, even though I was in bed, quite naked [*tout nu*]?" By both dreamy permissiveness and skeptical rigor (can I be sure I am not dreaming *now*?), the naked man may also be dressed. In oneiric telescoping and distortion, the man who is alternately naked or dressed, or in a way both at once, is

---

[3]See Derrida's review of Foucault's *Folie et deraison: Histoire de la folie à l'âge classique* (Paris: Plon, 1961) in *Writing and Difference*, trans. A. Bass (Chicago: University of Chicago Press, 1978), pp. 31–63.

exhibitionistic, or performs a striptease.[4] In any case, the narrator would be embarrassed, if interrogated, to explain so compromising a situation. Even when rarefied into epistemology, his situation is a continual molestation, and the narrator returns to it at the end of the *Meditations*, as if a major purpose of his writing—to clear himself of the suspicion of "dreaming"—had successfully been accomplished.

The effort of clearing himself may come too late, however. Descartes assures us that his dream doubts were "hyperbolic and ridiculous" (*M* 6) and can now, finally, be laughed off as a joke. But the doubts were already so designated in the second meditation, and the only new element to appear is that we are now assured a firm place from which to assess their excessiveness. Such assurance is suspect, however, because the author's coy teasing has been continual: recall the invitation for some readers but not others—who might be offended—to follow him along untrodden paths, or the invitation to close the eyes and go inward in an almost risqué liberation of thoughts from ordinary restraints (*D* 2, *M* 3). The Cartesian narrator protests a bit too much that what is innocuous and even salutary for him might not be so for all of us, that we will have to keep our minds clean of "prejudices," that the "authorities" might find moral errors in his text though he himself does not, that we ought not talk too much about what we learned from him but instead refer curious others to the text itself (*D* 2, 4, 6).

None of this, of course, need be (mis-)read as perverse or sexual, especially if we yield to the narrator's programmatic suggestions that although we are tearing down traditional

[4]With its dreams, its theatricalized domestic trappings, and a fantasized *mal ingénie*, Cartesian striptease is in the tradition which Roland Barthes describes: "evil is *advertised* the better to impede and exorcize it" [Barthes's italics] as part of a reassuring ritual in which there are "a whole series of coverings placed upon the body of the woman as . . . she pretends to strip it bare" ("Striptease," in *Mythologies*, trans. A. Lavers [New York: Farrar, Straus & Giroux, 1972], p. 84).

structures, we are still engaged in "discourse" or "meditations" about God and truth and are required, devoutly enough, to detach ourselves from our bodies. Yet the paradox that I am (in a way) and yet am not my body is surely a teaser. Our "I"—or Descartes's—is allegedly not body, though in the ending meditation (about the body and things) the "I", by a presumably nonhyperbolic trope, is "in" the body not "as a pilot in a ship" but *"tellement confondu et mêlé, que je compose comme un seul tout avec lui* [so blended and mixed that I compose a sort of unity with it]" (*M* 6). Note *comme*: the narrator, having valorized clarity and distinctness in the "natural light," nonetheless resorts to figures, which are always partly obscure or inapplicable. He resorts to them, moreover, at the very end of his implementation of an intellectual "method"—that is, at the point when they, or at least most of them, would seem entirely unnecessary.

To point to such seductive erroneousness is to challenge the notion propagated by both Descartes and certain of his modern commentators that Cartesian discourse is "demonstrative" rather than "rhetorical." When for example C. Perelman and L. Olbrechts-Tyteca align their *New Rhetoric* against Cartesian self-evidence,[5] they implicitly accept the dualism they purport to overcome, as do commentators who situate themselves according to a concern with either Descartes's "philosophy" or his "literary style" and historical place, but rarely with crossings of the two in his text's story and tactics of persuasion.[6] The text might be expected, of course, to suppress such crossings: the stress on self-evi-

[5] *The New Rhetoric* (Notre Dame: Notre Dame University Press, 1969), chap. 1.

[6] On the crossings, however, see for instance Georges Poulet, "Le songe de Descartes," in *Etudes sur le temps humain* (Paris: Plon, 1950); Theodor Spoerri, "La puissance métaphorique de Descartes," *Cahiers de Royaumont* 2 (Paris: Minuit, 1957):273–301; Robert Champigny, "The Theatrical Aspect of the Cogito," *Review of Metaphysics* 12 (1959):370–77; Nathan Edelman, "The Mixed Metaphor in Descartes," *Romanic Review* 41 (1950):167–78; Henri Gouhier, *La pensée métaphysique de Descartes* (Paris: Vrin, 1962), pp.

dence marks so strong a desire for persuasiveness that the tools of traditional rhetoric must become—so Descartes says—irrelevant.

On this issue comparisons are possible. Self-reform in Cartesian and Augustinian texts turns on a rejection of allegedly erroneous (or sinful) language in favor of unmediated (or less mediated) communications. Yet in both instances the text's own language cannot be transcended, and self-reform (especially of readers) becomes questionable. A precedent for the Cogito, as is often pointed out, may be located in Augustine: "How can I be mistaken that I am, since it is certain that I am, if I am mistaken? . . . Nor am I mistaken that I love, since I am not mistaken concerning the objects of my love. For, even though these objects were false, it would still be true that I loved illusions."[7] Descartes's version omits mention of love, and his narrator is more wary, distrustful, niggardly. The Cartesian "word" relies not on charity but on a self-evidence that will supposedly *force* assent (with all the appeal of violence) from even recalcitrant readers. No presumption is made that a citational or allegorical relation of the narrator's text to Scriptures would be convincing; on the contrary, citational tactics are rejected from the outset of the *Meditations*, since the "infidels" who are to be persuaded might suspect redundancy in requirements that "we must believe there is a God because we are so taught by the Holy Scriptures and . . . we must believe in the Holy Scriptures because they are from God" (*M*, pref.).

Descartes notices the infidel threat as he makes an appeal for ideological support: the "force" of his reasons will be ineffectual unless backed with the Sorbonne's "authority," in which case "I have no doubt, I say, that all errors and false

---

41–112; Sylvie Romanowski, *L'illusion chez Descartes* (Paris: Klincksieck, 1974).

[7] *City of God*, XI.26, trans. G. Walsh et al. (Garden City: Doubleday, 1958), p. 236.

opinions about those two questions [God and immortality] will soon be effaced from the minds of men" (*M*, ded.). His hyperbolic nondoubt is in this instance by no means self-evident, especially since he will soon indicate that he expects very few readers to be persuaded. In the "Preface to the Reader" his attitude is experimental: he will set forth the "considerations by which I persuade myself . . . in order to see if, by the same reasons that persuaded me, I can also persuade others." Note that Descartes frequently allows the "light of nature" to compel assent, although here—and virtually everywhere in the *Meditations*—he also speaks of "persuading" his readers or himself ("*je me persuade*"; "*je me suis persuadé*") (*M* 2, 3). He will not classify such efforts as "rhetoric," which he rejects as traditional, ornamental, and less persuasive than powerful reasoning spoken in even a low dialect (*D* 1). Taking his cue instead from clearly intuited objects, Descartes would evade the ambiguities of the linguistic sign.

Language, though, with its potentially disastrous ruses, is indispensable to his project. Even when he wishes to show how hyperbolic his doubt can become, all is doubted *except* the intelligibility of the words of doubting. At the moment of or before the Cogito, there should be no assurance of any meanings whatsoever, including linguistic meanings: as Derrida observes, the act of the Cogito in its hyperbolic moment of madness must be "distinguished from the language or the deductive system in which Descartes must inscribe it . . . for apprehension and communication."[8] Any such distinction, however, is of a Derridean slant; in the Cartesian text, the Cogito is staged *both* as naked thought *and* dressed in language. Here again we are teased: if at the moment of the Cogito, thinking and the saying of thinking can be uncritically equated, at other moments, especially after the Cogito,

[8]*Writing and Difference*, p. 59.

73

such an equation is less possible; thinking becomes hindered *in its saying* and so requires the indirection of tropes, testimonials, counterarguments, or self-censorship.

Indeed from one Cartesian text to another, as has been intimated, the requirements of language become increasingly vexatious. In the *Regulae* the narrator rejects syllogisms of the schools for containing their conclusions in their premises; such reasoning, which may explain and persuade (and can thus be relegated, he says, to "rhetoric"), cannot grasp the "truth of things" (*R* 10). His new rules, by contrast, will break with verbal obscurities by cutting off *his* verbal meanings from old meanings (*R* 3). The thematic thrust, to be reiterated elsewhere, is on the single author, as against the collecting or contesting of other authors. Although the single author in his independence can presumably minimize linguistic problems, the problems turn out to be merely displaced, since the author's independence (or distrust) will put him in an uneasy position with even himself. Not only does the narrator of the *Discourse on Method* "hate the profession of bookmaking," but the very act of writing is self-alienating: in his worry about possible controversy, he is "not able to put into my discourse all that I had in my mind" (*D* 5). How could this happen? Although in the remark's context, Descartes suggests that an awareness of others makes him beneficially self-corrective, that is but a fleeting moment of deference amid testy equivocations about authorial mission and readers' likely blindnesses (*D* 6). Could it be that the very act of disseminating "true" thoughts somehow makes them erroneous? Or that any ejaculation will be difficult and regrettable?

II

The Cartesian narrator's teasing is tied to an old intimacy with "error" or "deception," an intimacy that (contrary to the story's gist in both the *Discourse* and the *Meditations*) is always rhetorically useful and never finally relinquishable. The narrator's favorite mode, for example, is seductively self-representational: he thinks both *to* himself yet somehow *for*—and still more awkwardly, *to*—his readers. And he takes frequent stock, as he does so, of his intimacy with deception; even having raised his knowledge "to the highest possible point," it is possible that he is self-deceived (*"que je me trompe"*; *D* 1). He had been deceived "since infancy" by what he had been taught, particularly by and about "letters." With camouflaged (hence always deniable) irony, he offers perhaps purposely conventional praise for the books to which he was earlier, but now is no longer, subjected or enslaved (thus "as soon as I became of age to leave the subjection of my teachers, I gave up entirely the study of letters"; *D* 1).

In this, the Cartesian narrator's characteristic caution both heightens and qualifies his project's radicality. With doubts, for example, about books in general, what status can he confer upon the *Discourse* itself? In dubious deference to a reader's skepticism, Descartes (the anonymous author of its first publication) speaks of the *Discourse* as "a history, or, if you prefer, a fable," thus placing it—by his own criteria—among works valuable at best for entertainment but not to be trusted (*D* 1). Presumably readers will not be misled when warned that what they read is deceptive. Yet the author seems rhetorically intent on strengthening his position by weakening it, a paradox that opens a finely risky gap between author and reader: if we are rendered doubtful by or about our author, we become curious, perhaps even solicitous.

As that is happening, the narrator turns doubtfulness back: "almost all the world consists of [*n'est quasi composé que de*]" minds for which the text is entirely unsuitable: those impatient of method, or those who ought to follow the judgments of others (*D* 2). If this shelters the narrator, it places readers in a double bind: those who disqualify themselves are unable to assess the method, yet those who wish to avoid such disparagement are unable to dissent (modestly though the method seems to be offered) without suspicions of membership in the inferior class. Readers who refuse to take the double bind seriously, however, may reckon with it instead as an indication of the author-text relation: if the narrator urges a version of the mystique of authorship (cities are more beautiful when built by a single architect; *D* 2), the same insistence puts him—for he is only one author—in an uncomfortable position in setting forth his special claims: at the beginning of part 4, for instance, he suddenly and belatedly makes a direct address:

> I do not know that I ought to tell you [*vous*] of the first meditations made by me, for they are so metaphysical and so unusual that they may perhaps not be acceptable to everyone [*au goût de tout le monde*]. And yet at the same time, in order that one [*on*] may judge whether the foundations that I have laid are sufficiently secure, I find myself constrained in some measure to refer to them. [*D* 4]

Why the teasing reluctance? Are the "first" meditations too obviously the efforts of a novice? Or does the private narrator dread the dialogue he wishes to start? And why the succession of pronouns, *vous* suggesting an acquaintance that is immediately doubted in *on*? Such tactics of distancing become gradually more obtrusive, until they must be explained when the narrator offers a version of cosmic creation (in *Le Monde*) that he would not publish but that he paraphrases (as he painstakingly informs us) as the fiction of "a new world in an imaginary space" (*D* 5), that is, as a version of creation that he all along dissociates from Scriptures and that leads him to announce a hiatus between our minds and the world.

If the hiatus is to be overcome, he suggests, it must first be recognized: in the *Meditations* a major source of error is the naive belief that ideas come from "things outside of me which they entirely resemble" (*M* 3). Although the narrator thus suspends his belief in mimetic representation, he retains the inner/outer distinction according to which "error" can be rectified. A movement toward rectification, even so, is only apparently accomplished, and it corresponds somewhat marginally with such logocentric categories as "narrative," "logic," and even "self"-definition. This movement is entangled with a cluster of rhetorical difficulties. A "meditation" requires more attention than does a show or story and even perhaps (since its objects are different) than a mathematical proof. Yet the very requirement for special attentiveness from readers is suspect, even self-defeating: readers necessarily mis-meditate, since they only read-meditate or imagine themselves to meditate. In practice, indeed, the narrator is unable to maintain his announced brevity and self-sufficiency: beyond persuading himself and answering his own questions, he makes himself respond to the antagonistic objections of others, whose discourse becomes inelegantly tied to his own. The reader is directed from the outset to suspend judgment until finishing not only the text but the *Objections and Replies* (*M*, pref.). At some point well before that, though, he may wonder about how he "follows" the journey or—what is close—whether the narrator "progresses." A reader may follow in a number of ways: (1) certain—but possibly mistakenly certain—of perceiving by the "natural light," (2) uncertain of perceiving by the "natural light," (3) despite not perceiving by the "natural light." These joint possibilities may evoke anxiety, and a reader is likely to fasten critically upon some elements (conceptual mistakes, perhaps) by way of ignoring others. Since the narrator, too, may suffer anxiety, we might notice points where rhetorical (or "epistemological") tactics seem particularly urgent.

Here for instance is the beginning of the *Meditations*: "It is already some time ago that I perceived that, since my earliest years, I had received a quantity of false opinions as true" (*M* 1). The cognitive economy is in jeopardy; the narrator had been accepting (and perhaps circulating) counterfeits. Yet the counterfeits have become the normal currency, and "true" monies, presuming he could issue them, would themselves seem counterfeit. Although something must be done, the entire opening paragraph vacillates between the narrator's acquiescence to passing time and an alarm that at some point he must make an active break. Ordinary temporality is the region of uncontrollable error and deferral ("from my earliest years," "what made me defer for so long"), while the rupture of self-dismantling ("destroy . . . my old beliefs," "undo myself [*me défaire*]") is connected with a new temporality ("once in my life," "begin all over again"). Here as elsewhere, however, the figures are more impressive than, and they act as substitutes for, the stated motivations. Error and deception—which are, after all, unavoidable aspects of any ordinary life—are turned into formidable antagonists, so that a decisive struggle against them becomes a sort of heroism.

Although we may have a sense, then, that the narrator undertakes an epic or picaresque adventure, we are continually aware of the adventure's metaphoricity. Here a text supposedly of "philosophy," which makes claims to be truthful, appears more obviously fictional than "literature," which makes its claims indirectly—as puzzling allegory or mimetic realism.

Like the literary effort whose first requirement (says Henry James) is to be "interesting," the Cartesian project is continually threatened by—and must thus rhetorically provide for—the insubstantiality of its motivations and movements. If, more specifically, the Cartesian project is novelistic, so too are its problems. Descartes insists that there is a

Cartesian Striptease

useful method to his movements, yet the text operates in the
Shklovskian sense of typical atypicality:[9] even with its ties to
metaphysics and self-evidence, it disrupts—as much as and
more than most novels do—the habitual expectations of
logocentric readers. Its rhetoric is teasingly self-subversive:
the narrator appeals to the common man (in French) and to
the academics (in replies in Latin to the Objections) but also
excludes them both (he turns from the world to meditate, he
discourages unsuitable readers, he rejects books). The effect
is unsettling not only as a double bind but as a dramatized
oxymoron—solipsistic exhibitionism. The Cogito mentally
undresses "inside" to see what he (we) can find. The sexual
thrill intensifies the epistemological thrill, and conversely,
disinterested inquiry masks desire, or carnal knowledge. In
this hide-and-seek of improprieties, there can be no proper
ground; the imagery of wandering in the first two meditations is doubly metaphoric and turns out to be uncontrollably more powerful than the metaphors of well-made
foundations and straight roads that are meant subsequently
to displace them.

Recall the narrator in his initial, most exposed condition,
moving to arrive at this: "it is necessary to conclude, and to
hold as steadfast [*tenir pour constant*], that this proposition: *I
am, I exist* is necessarily true each time [*toutes les fois*] that I
pronounce it, or that I conceive it in my mind" (*M* 2). The
"truth" he says he can hold [*tenir*] is not holdable, for it is
"true" only at the disparate times of its performance and
"constant" only by presumption. Although the entire subsequent effort of the *Meditations* will be to overcome the discontinuity, that effort (as the objectors would insist in the
Objections and Replies) is less than persuasive: hyperbolic

[9]Victor Shklovsky, "Sterne's *Tristram Shandy*," in *Russian Formalist Criticism*, ed. L. Lemon and M. Reis (Lincoln: University of Nebraska Press,
1965), p. 57.

doubt once set loose, all certainties become illegitimate, and the objectors allow the semistripped stripper neither exit nor redress.

Such readers themselves, however, may have no exit: the narrator's recuperative efforts from the Cogito onward may seem gratuitously metaphysical or "merely" rhetorical, but then the readers' expectations for conventional narrative or discursive continuity must by all rights come into question as well. In ways that readers may prefer not to notice, the discontinuity of the Cogito is not overcome, or continuity is just as fictive as discontinuity. Could it be that with the Cogito's flickering perception-performance of "truth"—so apparently *unlike* truth—the Cartesian text makes its most exigent demands?

III

Let us return, as it seems we must, to the Cogito. Casting about for a "what" to fix himself, the Cogito rejects platitudes such as "rational animal," since they lead to endless verbal entanglements: each would have to be defined by another, "and so from a single question we would fall insensibly [*nous tomberions insensiblement*] into an infinity of others" (*M* 2). But is the alternative he proposes somehow *less* verbally entangling, *less* fallen? He had already "fallen," he says, into deep water (*M* 2), but with the Cogito he presumably begins to swim toward solid ground. He will "consider thoughts that are born [*naissent*] of themselves and inspired by my own nature" (*M* 2): these thoughts are supposedly neither definitions nor external, but close, unmediated, nondeceptive. Or so goes the dream that teases: the dressed narrator who is also naked here sees thoughts for which he, at least, needs no eyes.

But what might have happened between the moment of seeing and the moment of writing (speaking)? Has he forgotten his surprise, in the *Discourse*, at finding a hiatus even when thinking? Although he seems able to avoid the question of how thoughts "belong" to me or "me" to thoughts, he cannot avoid the impression, even by adding attributes to "thinking" (affirming, denying, doubting, etc.), of a temporal disjunction of "me," the thinker. The thinker on the one hand recognizes discontinuity as a condition of ordinary life *hidden by* sentimental stories of continuity, against which is juxtaposed, "*I am, I exist*, but for how long? [*pour combien de temps?*]" (*M* 2). He presses, on the other hand, for a continuity which is more assured than that of ordinary life. If divisibility defines body as against mind (*M* 6), the temporal division of the Cogito ("my life can be divided into an infinity of parts") (*M* 3) must be hypothetical or metaphoric, as shown by a God who is ostensibly neither hypothetical nor metaphoric but proven. The thinking self cannot author its continuity, but it can "see"—again without eyes—that there is a perfect God who does so ("it is necessary that God be the author of my existence, because all the time of my life can be divided"; *M* 3). Like the narrator, however, the Cartesian God is somewhat of a teaser. He is "known" by an idea but is nonetheless incomprehensible (as the infinite; *M* 3). And he is argued for by questions: "Now it is manifest by the natural light that there must be at least as much reality in the efficient and total cause as in its effect: for whence can the effect draw its reality if not from its cause? And how could this cause communicate its reality, if the cause did not have it in itself?" (*M* 3). The questions must be rhetorical or figurative (God and the narrator are metonymically related), for if taken grammatically or literally, they may have no answer.

The objectors were slowest to follow at approximately this point, if indeed not earlier. How can we tell, they asked, *when* we perceive clearly and distinctly? And "what evidence is there that you are not deceived and cannot be deceived when you have clear and distinct knowledge?" (*O* 2). Within the self, Descartes responds, perception and "persuasion" may be simultaneous (*RO* 2). What happens, however, when other selves must be persuaded? Here Descartes refuses to allow that there may be error or even disagreement when selves "draw the clearness of their vision from the intellect alone" (*RO* 2). Ideally, what is clear and distinct for the narrator is equally so for the reader; the first-person form enables the reader easily to identify his "I" with the narrator's. Yet a reader, who at some point may no longer follow the plot, might cease further identification—quite possibly with a feeling that he, like the early narrator himself, had been deceived. He might even say, with Father Bourdin, "*You say, 'I am.' I deny it. You proceed: 'I think.' I deny it*" (*O* 8). This statement is not mere petulance, and it can be related to a more general point: meditation may have made the author's perceptions so exceptional as to isolate him not only from the senses but from the world of common discourse (*O* 2). "*You have for so many years so exercised your mind by continual meditation, that matters which to others seem doubtful and obscure are to you most certain*" (*O* 2). The objectors require—mockingly, it seems—that "*the principle of clear and distinct knowledge should be explained . . . clearly and distinctly*" (*O* 2). They pose in effect an authorial problem, and Descartes specifies tactics: he used the looser mode of "analysis," which "contains nothing to incite belief in an inattentive or hostile reader," whereas he might, if he wished, have used the more rigorous mode of "synthesis," in which "the reader, however hostile and obstinate, is compelled to render his assent" (*RO* 2). Aggression against hostile readers of the *Meditations*, however, might not be triumphant, since the compulsion is admittedly not geometric ("geometrical proofs harmonize with the use of our senses, and are readily granted by all, . . . [whereas] in metaphysics nothing causes more trouble than making the perception of its primary notions clear and distinct"; *RO* 2).

Here again the linguistic sign blocks: to have readers, the

narrator must use language, infested though it be with prejudices. He claims, at times, to move from linguistic to conceptual categories: in one reply he agrees that St. Thomas
Aquinas had argued that "*when the meaning of the word God is
understood, it is understood that God exists,*" but he distinguishes
his argument from St. Thomas's as depending not on words
but on understanding: "we clearly and distinctly understand
that to exist belongs to His true . . . nature; therefore we
can with truth affirm of God that he exists" (*RO* 1). Not only
is this linguistically mediated, however, but the narrator himself grants (later) that something self-evident may be merely
his own: "though to me it is very certain [that mind and
body are distinct], I do not promise that others can be convinced of the same truth however attentive they are and, in
their own judgment, clear-sighted" (*RO* 6). How, then, is the
author's claim to truth more legitimate than counterclaims?
To mandates that his readers be unprejudiced and attentive,
the Cartesian narrator's readers could—and did—suggest
that the fault might not be theirs but his: "*we have read what
you have written seven times and have, so far as in us lay, given an
attention to it equal to that of the Angels, and have nevertheless not
yet been convinced*" (*O* 6). They urge him to reword what
seems verbally obscure, but apparently with an anticipation
of his failure.

On the level of plot, furthermore, objector-readers might
speculate that the narrative movement of the *Meditations* is
self-undermining not only as metaphysics but as a story flat-
tened by rationalistic simplifications. Although any such critique depends on notions of a "story" as organic and contin-
uous, the text itself may nourish such notions with signs of
post-Cogito recuperations and continuity. Misled by misleading promises of conclusiveness, we may thus, like many of
the objectors, enter into quarrels that are irrelevant not because of any lack of intellectual cogency but because clues
had all along been scattered (for which the narrator had no

eyes) that the plot would move divergently from its itinerary (as stated in the Synopsis, say, or just before meditations 5 and 6).

Consider an instance of alleged nondivergence, when the narrator who allows his mind to wander unconstrained by "the correct limits [*justes bournes*] of truth" finds himself nonetheless "insensibly [*insensiblement*] returned to where I wished" (*M* 2), even though "insensibly" he is usually led into error ("I fall back insensibly . . ."; "insensibly into error"; *M* 2). In this instance the narrator obtains a piece of wax and places it before the fire (in the same study, no doubt, where we visit him) so that it melts and its sensory qualities are all changed. This metamorphosis of the wax is offered as a brief story ("its color changes, it loses its shape, it grows larger, it liquefies") and yet is denied for the same reason as disclosing what the wax really "is". Presumably to the still erring mind (unconstrained by "truth") the story does offer a kind of knowledge, however trite, about the wax. Yet if that mind is limited, here again, to ordinary ways of looking, it has missed another story, which is that, having "taken off its clothes, I consider [the wax] completely naked [*toute nue*]" (*M* 2).

Nakedness is traditionally an icon for prelapsarian purity, while postlapsarian nakedness is covered. Here the tease— about a tease—is that we need two sets of eyes, and that proper and improper seeing are reversible: the senses, including bodily eyes (*la vision des yeux*) apprehend sensual qualities but are in error, while a nonbodily "inspection of the mind" sees nakedness and is itself (we observed) virtually naked. The narrator gives us an apparently innocent story and then takes it back as being dangerously unreliable even as he tells us that the same story—or perhaps for propriety's sake, no story at all—is far more "true" if we notice that its protagonist is being gradually undressed. But which sort of mind or pair of eyes, we might ask, is the more wandering or erring?

Cartesian Striptease

The doubleness of the wax story seems indeed to reiterate a doubleness (duplicity, perhaps) in the Cogito moment, when a narrator skilled at self-suspending seems very much himself even while claiming that his usual life has been set aside: "I had persuaded myself that here was nothing at all in the world, that there was no heaven, no earth, no wind, no bodies; but was I then not also persuaded that I did not exist? No indeed, I exist" (*M* 2). With a characteristic resentment of "external" irritations (language, books, bodies, readers), the narrator is here at perhaps his most comfortable—hyperbolic, false, fictional, but also, of course, "true." He seems, indeed, all the more "true" (to his situation) the less he controls it, and the final meditations—which ostensibly defigure hyperbole and reinstate mimetic signs—will only reaffirm such a possibility.

In the sixth meditation, for instance, when the narrator enters into what he designates as the dangerously erroneous area of sense perception, he shows that his body is (in a way) "outside" of him, and he thus speaks knowingly of its erroneousness without having to commit himself. He continues his striptease, in other words, by speaking directly of experiences of corporeal pleasures, pains, appetites, illnesses, and wounds, even while insisting that the body is not (yet is) "him" (*M* 6). Since he offers to resolve his hyperbole (about having no body and no world) only to replace it, as we remarked, with yet other figures, the deceptiveness of bodily functions may have entered perforce into his now ostensibly "true" discourse. The tease of rhetorical substitutions is that the body with its errors functions as no more than the narrator's clothing, so that if he *takes off his body* he can never be accused of sexual impropriety (if that is bodily), and when he puts his body back on, as he does, so to speak, in meditation 6, he "covers" himself by arguing that it is not really "him"—that is, the Cogito.

In and despite such rhetorical switches, the narrator's language may uncontrollably undo him. The explicit story in the *Meditations* is of an increasing awareness of what the narrator can know and of how he can control error. But if the story of the wax (of not "knowing") was also a counterstory, so too is this story (of "knowing"), and as it concludes, the narrator is particularly vigilant about gaps of communication. He reinstates mimetic representation: ideas of corporeal things "must" (lest God be a deceiver) come from corporeal things, even though our perceptions are necessarily "very obscure and confused" (*M* 6). All sorts of distortions, he warns, are possible, not only in transfers between "outer" and "inner" regions but even "inside" his body, whose message system is notably unreliable (a pain in the foot must traverse various anatomical parts before reaching the brain, and may be impeded anywhere along the way or misinterpreted even when it arrives; *M* 6). The body's interest, moreover, is in finding pleasure rather than truth, and its signifying operations are likely to be perverted: "sense perceptions being placed in me to signify to my mind which things are suitable and which damaging [*convenables et nuisibles*], . . . I nevertheless use them as if they were rules to know bodies" (*M* 6).

The narrator tries to alleviate this situation by noting his habit of (mis-)reading bodily signals as though they could provide cognition. Yet even if genuine cognition be relegated to mental illuminations, the Cogito's composition as fictive language reiterates supposedly "corporeal" perceptual gaps and interventions. Precisely these gaps and interventions, moreover, are the unacknowledged force for epistemological pretensions. Thus meditations 5 and 6, which tell or error and its control, do so not only by providing examples of error but by becoming erroneous and in some (possibly deceptive) ways conceding so. Consider the narrator's hasty reassembling of the world he had so painstakingly suspended: "My senses signal to me [*me signifient*] more usually [*ordinairement*] what is true than what is false about things that are or are not advantageous to the body [*les commodités du corps*]" (M 6). Is this part of the "truth," then, that the narrator-epistemologist had set out to find and that he earlier seemed to promise? Suspiciously akin to the flickering performative of his Cogito, it seems radically other than traditionally abiding truth. Or (to move only slightly further) the narrator has hardly separated corporeal perception from noncorporeal perception in the "natural light," since the second works by analogy to the first. The narrative indeed suggests, despite contrary claims, that *commodités* may twist the "truth" of all perceptions or—since *commodités* can never definitively be set aside—that "truth" is erroneous.

With just such erroneous truth, even so, the Cartesian narrator offers to "conjoin past and present knowledges [*connaissances*]" and to dismiss his erstwhile doubts as "hyperbolic and ridiculous" (M 6). We need not be tempted by this offer or by pieties as to "the infirmity and the weakness of our nature" (M 6), since they, as much as any of our own expectations for "logic" or a coherent "story," may deflect attention from textual rhetoricity as an ungroundable series of tropings. Faced with such tropings, we may be solicitous to out-doubt the doubter, so as thereafter to slip back into our everyday adventures and stories. But beyond a certain point of Cartesian rereading, will that always be a possibility?

4

Deconstructing Authors:
Don Quixote

> I asked him what he was laughing at, and he responded
> that it was something written in the margin.
>
> —*Don Quixote*

In episode after episode, *Don Quixote* raises radical
questions about signs and desire—often under the relatively
innocent guise of skepticism about perception and belief.
Commentators have to some extent recognized these questions, which they nonetheless domesticate sooner or later by
appeals to various unifying concepts—mimesis of "life" or
the hidden will of an author—even though (indeed perhaps
because) precisely such concepts are under constant
interrogation.

Take for instance the notion of authorial will. Martín
de Riquer has recently offered statistical evidence that serious critiques of the chivalric romances were being made
throughout the sixteenth century, and that thus the prologue to *Don Quixote* is not anachronistic in its stated aim of
mocking the romances. Riquer's thesis is considerably weakened, however, in that he assumes that the prologue author
and other characters speak for or "coincide with" Cervantes.[1] Such an assumption is particularly astonishing when

[1]"Cervantes y la caballeresca," in *Suma Cervantina*, ed. J. B. Avalle-Arce
and E. C. Riley (London: Tamesis, 1973): "Miguel de Cervantes professes
so many times that he writes *Don Quixote* in order to . . ." (p. 282); "Cervantes, who at various times, coincides with this opinion . . ." (p. 282); "the

made in regard to a text in which one of the crucial themes is that authors constantly misrepresent their subjects and themselves.

Even commentators with somewhat more subtle arguments still appear inclined toward what might be called the mystique of authorship. Ángel del Río uses the term "perspectivism" for the text's doubtfulness and for its allowance of various readings, but he ends by stressing that "Cervantes creates the permanent model for all novelistic heroes."[2] Although a glorification of the author is relatively subdued here, in other commentators it becomes a key motif. Recall Leo Spitzer's essay "Linguistic Perspectivism in the *Quixote*," which notes the text's polynomasia and linguistic ambivalences: "words . . . are, like the books in which they are contained, sources of hesitation, error, deception— dreams."[3] From this broad textual bemusement, Spitzer finds a way to affirm—Cartesianly, as he recognizes—what he presumes to be the enormous powers of the authorial cogito: "High above this world-wide cosmos of his making, . . . Cervantes' artistic self is enthroned, an all-embracing creative self, Naturelike, Godlike, almighty, all-wise, all-good—and benign."[4] Granted Spitzer's perspectivistic premises, his movement to this conclusion is hardly compelling, since precisely authorship in *Don Quixote* is depicted as fallible and mendacious—that is, as anything but "Godlike."

Spitzer even so is not alone in his attitude. Alban K. Forcione, after arguing for "Cervantes' suspicion of the fundamental direction of sixteenth-century critical thought, which would institutionalize . . . Aristotle's conception of imitation," infers that "for Cervantes the artist stands beyond all

---

explicit purpose of the great novel, so often stressed by Cervantes . . ." (p. 286; my translations).

[2]"El Equívoco del 'Quijote,'" *Hispanic Review* 27 (1959):221.

[3]*Linguistics and Literary History: Essays in Stylistics* (Princeton: Princeton University Press, 1948), p. 52.

[4]*Ibid.*, pp. 69, 73.

the norms and restrictions by which criticism would control his creative powers, as god above both his creation and his audience."[5] Only by a misleading logic can an attack on mimetic doctrines lead to a liberation from them,[6] and few texts acknowledge this more thoroughly than does *Don Quixote*. Forcione nonetheless privileges the author, as do other commentators. F. W. Locke, after showing how the authors in *Don Quixote* are all unreliable, writes that "Cervantes himself is an image of God"; Mia Gerhardt, in a comparable demonstration, contends that "Cervantes, beneath his multiple masks, affirms his creative omnipotence"; Ruth El Saffar, after arguing that "distance is the prerequisite for artistic control," moves to the conclusion that "it is the hidden, implied author who can be seen to have absolute artistic control."[7] Here as elsewhere, one need not be tempted by what might seem to be offered. Cervantes has no more or less "control" over his text than does any other writer; he is not a hidden god, and his power is "absolute" at most rhetorically, that is, in comparison with that of his fictional authors. What I shall argue indeed is that the text's intertextual rela-

---

[5]*Cervantes, Aristotle and the Persiles* (Princeton: Princeton University Press, 1970), p. 125. Forcione later notes, however, that poets in Cervantes "are tainted with criminality; they glory not in the act of edification but rather in the act of deception; any supernatural connections which they may have are infernal" (p. 306).

[6]See Jacques Derrida, "Economimesis," trans. R. Klein, *Diacritics* 11, no. 2 (1981):3–25.

[7]F. W. Locke, "El Sabio Encantador: The Author of *Don Quixote*," *Symposium* 23 (1969):59; Mia Gerhardt, *Don Quijote: La vie et les livres* (Amsterdam: Noord-Hollandsche Uitg. Mij., 1953), p. 33; Ruth S. El Saffar, "The Function of the Fictional Narrator in *Don Quijote*," *Modern Language Notes* 83 (1968):175–76. See also Marthe Robert, *The Old and the New*, trans. C. Cosman (Berkeley: University of California Press, 1977), pp. 167–68: *Don Quixote* gives "proof that literature can only endlessly repeat its dreams, and if the writer is wrong to mistake this repetition for immortality, at least he has the unique privilege of catching himself openly in his own error." But the writer's "error catching" (which may not occur "openly") is often already inscribed in the repeated dream, and—so regarded—"he" becomes far less privileged.

tions are not simply satirical or even parodic, that authorship in *Don Quixote* is questioned in all its dimensions, including reading.

I

In an inconclusive discussion—one of many—over the merits of the chivalric romances, someone in *Don Quixote* recounts the performance of an exemplary knight who attacked an army of over a million armed soldiers, and "routed them all as if they had been flocks of sheep" (1.32).[8] The hyperbolic simile is conventional enough and is made in passing, but a reader will readily recall that one of Don Quixote's first knightly endeavors is to attack what he sees as armed soldiers, which then turn out to be flocks of sheep (1.18). The transformation of one version of the story into its inversion is less chivalrically significant, it seems, than the association of one version with the other; this being so, there can be no objective or nontropological criterion as to which of them is the more "heroic" or "knightly" or "original," and the work of apparently damaging figures—enchanters or "authors"—unavoidably partakes of knightly affairs.

No mastery, least of all by authors, seems possible over such endless mimetic proliferation. Recall how the prologue author appears as "himself" in a posture of suspense, "the paper in front of me, my pen in my ear" (1 prol., tm). Productively askew—pen in ear—he is self-inseminating; is this belied or not by his just having extensively written? He has nothing "to cite in the margins," and his nonmargined writing, he worries, is not a book: he follows no *auctores* and so

---

[8]References to *Don Quixote* are by part and chapter in the J. M. Cohen translation (Baltimore: Penguin, 1950); Spanish citations are from the edition of Martín de Riquer (Barcelona: Juventúd, 1965). At several points "tm" indicates that Cohen's translation has been modified.

The Rhetoric of Doubtful Authority

(he says) cannot add their names to—or next to—his text. A mere glance at *Don Quixote*, however, would promptly inform a reader of all sorts of textual and authorial names (Amadís de Gaula, Antonio de Lofraso, Don Alonso de Ercilla, etc.; 1.6). Presumably none of these are worthwhile, and indeed the prologue author's "purpose"—his *mira*—is "to undo" (*deshacer*—dismantle, unmake) "their authority and influence" (1 prol.).

Since his own (non-)book, however, can have no citable support from *auctores* (such as, he says, Plato, Aristotle, or the Scriptures), its very struggle must be, he suggests, marginal. His whole project, indeed, is overdetermined: (1) the prologue author is "too spiritless and lazy to go about looking for authors" yet nonetheless needs them and does at any rate refer to Homer, Ovid, Scriptures (1.32, 49, 2.22); (2) he can easily make up deceptive references yet writes the kind of book that requires none, though such notions (and the statement of *mira*) are offered not by him but by his "friend"; (3) the *mira*, as in *mirar*, is the way something looks, as in "mirror," "miracle," "mirage."[9] Such features are quixotic, re-marking—in Derrida's term, *hors livre*—the undecidability of mimesis as a possibly "productive" doubling in "representation" and a possibly non- or pseudoproductive

---

[9]All these are derived, according to the OED, from the same Latin root. For *mira* as a noun the Royal Spanish Academy lists a number of military and visual meanings: it is what might provide a target for seeing; in ancient fortresses it is an elevated place that allows for a sight of the surrounding terrain; it is also a variable star of the constellation of the Whale (Real Academia Española, *Diccionario* [Madrid: Espasa Calpe, 1970]). The classical Latin *mirare* is "(1) to wonder, be astonished at . . . , (2) to admire, look on with admiration" (*Cassell's New Latin Dictionary* [New York: Funk & Wagnalls, 1959]). In medieval Latin, according to the British Academy's *Revised Medieval Latin Word List* (London: Oxford, 1965), *mirifico* is "to magnify, make wonderful," and Eric Partridge in *Origins: A Short Etymological Dictionary of Modern English* (London: Routledge, 1958), p. 408, traces the following linkages: "*miracle, miraculous; mirage; mirific; mirror* (n, hence v);—*admire* (whence *admirer*), *admirable, admiration, admirative*;—*marvel* (n,v), *marvellous.—smile*, v (whence agent *smiler* and pa, vn *smiling*) hence n;—prob of *smirk*, v (whence *smirker* and *smirking*) hence n."

doubling in deceptive similitudes, sorcery, masks, or personae.[10]

Genealogically productive doubling is from the outset doubted even as it is affirmed; the prologue author, in his alleged difference from everyone else, seems neither inside nor outside the natural order, which, he claims, confines him:

> Idle reader: you can believe without any oath of mine that I would wish this book, as the son of my brain [*hijo del entendimiento*], to be the most beautiful, the liveliest and the cleverest imaginable. But I have not been able to contravene the order of nature by which each thing engenders its similar [*semejante*]. So what could my sterile and ill-cultivated genius engender [*engendrar . . . el ingenio mío*] except the story of a son who is dry, shrivelled, capricious, full of varied thoughts that no one else has ever imagined . . . ? [1 prol., tm]

The supposedly "natural" father-son connection is indeed (or nonetheless) displaced by an author-work connection and even there, playfully, by a lesser one: "I, though apparently Don Quixote's father, am his stepfather" and thus will not implore the reader's indulgence toward "this, my [now metaphoric?] son" (*ibid.*, tm). However this may be, if the (step-)father-son, author-product relation is of naming, the author in his concern for referential truth will not decide which among various possible names—Quejada, Quesada, etc.—is Don Quixote's "real" or "original" name, especially since the names do not matter for what he calls the "truth of the story" (1.1). This is in a way repeated: the author's *semejante* "invents" in his madness names that are nonetheless always quasi-referential (del Toboso, Rocin-ante).

Suspicion may be thereby cast, however, on the self-styled beginning author who performs his role by determining "correct" references and by providing assurances (to the be-

[10]*La dissémination* (Paris: Seuil, 1972), pp. 211–13. See also Cesáreo Bandera, *Mimesis conflictiva* (Madrid: Gredos, 1975).

ginning reader) that Don Quixote misperceives ("That was in fact the road our knight actually took"; ". . . that was the truth"; "The case . . . is this"; 1.2, 28, 21). Any simple allocation of "truth" to the author and "error" to the protagonist becomes, in this story, increasingly untenable, since (as we learn) there seems to be no first or final or dominating author, and even if there were one (Cervantes has been given the title), he for all his *ingenio* would possess no virgin signifieds to become signifiers, no subject not already engendered. And if any viewpoint—any story, emotion, project, *mira*—may be visible from another, less committed (or more mocking) viewpoint, the second is not more or less valuable than the first, nor can their relation be described in such terms as subordination, incorporation, validity, or truth.

There can be, then, no mimetic—and incidentally, deselving—proliferation from which any author may be protected, however far "outside" (or "inside") the text he may seem to situate himself; thus the naively confident discriminations of the beginning author are strikingly changed when "his" manuscript is ruptured: "The author of this history left the battle in suspense at this critical point, with the excuse that he could find nothing else written about these deeds of Don Quixote than the ones already given. It is true that the second author of this work did not wish to believe that such a curious history could be consigned to the laws of forgetfulness [*olvido*]" (1.8, tm). We are confronted again with a questionableness of authorship. Who is the "second" author? Did the narrator somehow become entitled, at this point, a "second author" and how is he an "author" rather than an editor or copier? Indeed, with his dependence on always prior manuscripts, why is he "second" rather than third, fourth, or *x*th? On the other hand, if he "did not want to believe" in the text's *olvido* amid evidence of the interrupted activities of prior authors, might he in some respects have made himself an inventor (author?) of Don Quixote's futher adventures?

Having assumed, after all, a disdainful attitude toward the knight's madness, he suddenly reverses himself and praises "the light and mirror, . . . our gallant Don Quixote," and so on (1.9), as if worried at the manuscript's fragility. Apparently compensating for his earlier stance, the second author (if "he" is "the same") both questions that stance and makes himself its satiric object. His deferral as "second" author to another, however, is comparably unclear: he announces the Arab historian as the "first" author only to designate him a liar and to exercise power over him by an application of norms: "when he could and should have extended the *pluma* [feather or pen] in praises of so fine a knight, he seems painstakingly to have passed them by in silence; a thing poorly done and worse thought out, since historians are obliged to be precise, truthful and objective" (1.9, tm). "Truth," then, is located in what might seem (or had seemed shortly before) to be erroneous or hyperbolic, while deception is located in a report of merely historical facts.

Here as elsewhere in *Don Quixote*, apparently rhetorical writing is deemed "truer" than apparently nonrhetorical writing which for the same reason becomes troped. Any "truth of the story" (to use a recurrent phrase) is itself a story, any norm by which "rhetoric" or "authorship" might be assessed is itself rhetorical or authorial. If the stepfather-author can never quite be aligned with his hero or text (or the prologue author with traditional *auctores*), the text's own authors, too, are always fissured by supplementarity: each author—"first" or "second"—becomes secondary to the other. Recall for instance: "they say that the proper original [*el propio original*] of this history reads that when Cide Hamete came to write this chapter his interpreter did not translate it as written" (2.44, tm). The author who could have written and known this distances the text's production without thereby substituting "his" production as a new present. The "*propio original*" is necessarily both more and less authoritative than that of Cide Hamete and the translator: it is self-perpetuating, legendary, fictional—the amusingly impossible basis (since it includes their deviations) for what Cide Hamete and the translator write. It suspiciously resembles the "present" history, thus locating itself further from rather than closer to the "original." Authors like those of *Don Quixote*, who defend or protest their plight, question the text as they produce it: the translator finds that Cide Hamete, though he cherishes the Montesinos episode, notes in the margin that he cannot quite believe it, and so merely inscribes it apart from truth or falsity (2.24). "Truth" then is marginal, if that, yet only in the margins (which the prologue author was reluctant to mark with *auctores*) can an authorial *ingenio* be momentarily disclosed in "original" exclamations about the possible irrelevance of truth.

The marginality is undecidably mimetic: authorial writing is marginal to the "central" story even though that story, diagetically, is marginal to its inscriptions. Distinctions such as author/character and story/text continually reverse themselves or coalesce. How far, then, can quixotic "error" be separated from the erroneous writing about it, or when, if ever, is the error/truth binary telling? The text that endlessly rehearses such questions can only concur with the quixotic attitude that referential truth is more a "rhetorical" than an "epistemological" necessity, although it is both. Recall the quixotic attitude: cognitive errors are rarely of concern, for even when Don Quixote recognizes them, they often confirm his knighthood (in the work of envious enemies) or are not "his" as a knight. He thus is angry when Sancho, who laughs at the fulling-mills mistake, fails to perceive the irrelevance of error: "Am I, by chance, obliged, being as I am a knight, to recognize and distinguish sounds, and know whether they are fulling-hammers or not?" (1.20). And of course the "enchanters" who (Don Quixote claims) transform appearances are repeatedly held responsible for errors.

If on the one hand, however, Don Quixote disparages certain errors, he is extremely punctilious, on the other hand, about "correct" referentiality in narratives and about the "correct" enunciation of words (e.g., 1.12). Thus even as he admits that (owing to enchantment) he cannot always venture correct perceptual judgments, he also insists that a certain kind of language—chivalric language—is necessarily referential. He thus judges that what seems a barber's basin must be a helmet, though he defers judgment on the pack-saddle/harness question, which is not in his area of authority (1.45). The very quality of knightly discourse "must," he claims, validate certain of his judgments and actions, and even if they should go askew, that by no means detracts from the discourse that defines them. This notion, so seemingly foolproof, will nonetheless be put into question. For the quixotic mission, as Michel Foucault has shown, proposes to revise a temporal process: the signs of chivalric language, if they are out of conformity with the "present" world, might by certain actions and discourse (Don Quixote believes) be forced into closer conformity.[11] The effort to reconnect discontinuities, however, eventually proves futile, and the quixotic sign is at the same time deconstructed.

The possibilities for deconstruction can perhaps be noted in the situations that Don Quixote seems anxious to overcome. Recall his beginning experiments (echoing the prologue author's) to legitimize himself. He needs to be dubbed and to have a squire, and he soon fulfills both requirements. There remain, even so, requirements that he cannot so easily accomplish but that he hopes can nonetheless be fulfilled. He needs an author (though not immediately) and he needs

[11]Michel Foucault, *The Order of Things* (New York: Pantheon, 1970), pp. 46–77.

(though, he says, only perhaps) a genealogy. His problem is that having erased one self so as to invent another, he by-passes the generative—if not the authorial—process, and his referential marks (Quixote, La Mancha) are vague beyond genealogical usefulness. The ancestral armor that might have heraldically signaled his lineage is "eaten with rust and mouldy," and in any case the prospective knight cleans it into plainness, later overlaying upon it his emblem of the "*triste figura*" (1.1), as if inscribing an engendering out of signs only as ancestors.

Such an effort becomes an obstacle in his paradigmatic narrative according to which a knight, after distinguishing himself to the point where he might marry a princess, must nonetheless offer proof of royal blood. Here is Don Quixote's statement, in part, of the paradigm:

> A knight must wander through the world, on probation as it were, looking for adventures, so that if he achieves a few, he will gain such name and fame that when he arrives at the court of some great monarch, he will already be well-known by his deeds. Then as soon as the boys see him ride through the city gates, they will all follow him and surround him and shout: "Here is the Knight of the Sun!"—or of the Serpent, or of any other device under which he may have performed his great deeds. . . . The King himself will come half-way down his staircase, embrace him most warmly, greet him, kiss him on the cheek, and lead him to the chamber of his lady Queen. There the knight will find her with the Princess, her daughter, who is sure to be one of the loveliest and most perfect damsels to be found anywhere. . . . She will gaze into the knight's eyes and he into hers, and each will seem to the other rather divine than human. [1.21, tm]

The knight, to prove himself further, will then fight a successful battle against one of the king's enemies. There will be some question, even so, of the knight's genealogical qualifications for marriage to a princess, and Don Quixote worries about his (non-)origins: "I do not know how it can be proved that I am of royal blood, or even second cousin to an Emperor" (1.21). He can only wish that "the sage who comes to write my history will so establish my parentage and descent that I shall find I am fifth or sixth in descent from a King" (1.21). Any so-called genealogy, however, might not be established, and Don Quixote tries to evade requirements: his heroic deeds will outweigh his lineage, or perhaps the princess will love him so much that, despite her father, she will "take me for her lord and husband, even though she clearly knows I am the son of a water-carrier," and should there still be obstacles, he will simply carry her off (1.21).

II

Caught up as he is in this particular story, Don Quixote seems to forget that he has already dealt with the problem, so to speak, in the figure of Dulcinea as his lady and princess. The possible advantage here is the referential "del Toboso," which Don Quixote attaches to her name, as if expecting that the more completely he becomes a knight, the more completely can she become a princess. Such a possibility, indeed, he seems keen to put to the test.

The quixotic project so conceived, we might observe, parallels both Augustine's effort to communicate with God and Descartes's to prove God's existence, for in the knight's system, "Dulcinea" performs the rhetorical function that "God" does in theirs. The issue is complicated, however, in that traditional Petrarchan metaphoric transferences (as Don Quixote suggests to Sancho) are not merely reiterated, but used:

> Do you think that the Amaryllises, the Phyllises, Sylvias, Dianas, Galateas, Phyllidas, and all the rest . . . were really flesh-and-blood ladies and the mistresses of the writers who wrote about them? Not a bit of it. . . . I am quite satisfied, therefore, to imagine and believe that the good Aldonza Lorenzo is lovely

99

and virtuous; her family does not matter a bit, [and] . . . I think of her as the greatest princess in the world. [1.25]

So he says—at this point. Yet Don Quixote not only invokes Dulcinea's power for the performance of each exploit but demands, with each "triumph," that the victims *visit* her. Although such requests meet with confused resistance or with merely promised compliance, Don Quixote no doubt comes under the impression, even so, that as the triumphs, requests, and visits add up, "Dulcinea" must somehow become more fully referential. Thus when Sancho returns from a commissioned visit to her, Don Quixote is solicitously attentive to the most minute details: adapting himself to Sancho's way of thinking, he on the one hand allegorizes the lady's qualities out of Sancho's earthy remarks but on the other seems to "believe" more strongly than ever in her empirical actuality:

> ". . . Go on," said Don Quixote. "You got there; and what was that queen of beauty doing? I am sure that you found her stringing pearls, or embroidering a device with thread of gold for this, her captive knight."
> "No, she wasn't doing that," replied Sancho, "but winnowing a couple of bushels of wheat in her back yard."
> "Then you can be certain," said Don Quixote, "that the grains of that wheat turned to pearls at the touch of her hand."

And a bit further on:

> "Well, then," continued Don Quixote, "she has finished winnowing her corn and sent it to the mill. What did she do when she had read my letter?"
> "She didn't read the letter," said Sancho, "for she said she couldn't read or write. . . . She said it was quite enough that I had told her by word of mouth about your worship's love for her." [1.31]

What Sancho thus delivers as the "communication" of an unwriting Dulcinea requires, Don Quixote learns, the more direct communication of a visit: "She ended up by telling me to tell your worship that she kissed your hands, and that she had far rather see you than write to you" (1.31). Although he is willing to oblige, Don Quixote has scruples: Sancho's trip was suspiciously fast, and so some enchanter (like a sophist, or a narrator of fictions) must have shortened temporal-spatial dimensions: "you [Sancho] have only taken three days travelling to El Toboso and back, and it is a good ninety miles. . . . I conclude that the sage necromancer, who is my friend, and looks after my affairs—for I certainly have [one], . . . must have assisted you on your journey without your knowing it" (1.31). Don Quixote links referential problems to a sage necromancer: one calls up the other. But he may protest a bit too much that the enchanter is helpful, friendly, and part of the knight's self, since almost everywhere else enchanters are hostile, envious, and unreliable.

Enchanters are like the Cartesian *mal ingénie*: deceive Don Quixote how they may, they cannot subvert his chivalric courage.[12] This situation is far less assured, however, than that of the Cartesian narrator, for with Sancho's problematic "enchantment" of Dulcinea, the evil demons insinuate themselves into the Quixotic Cogito itself, beclouding its natural light. Don Quixote, searching for Dulcinea's abode, must rely (much more than he usually does) upon the guidance of Sancho, who has "seen" the lady. Yet as Sancho worries quietly about where in El Toboso to go, and suddenly announces that one of three approaching peasant girls "is" the lady Dulcinea, Don Quixote harbors doubts, and warns San-

---

[12]Cartesian and Cervantine resemblances have been widely noticed: Spitzer points to *Don Quixote* as a precursor of the *Discourse on Method* (*Linguistics and Literary History*, p. 69); Américo Castro speculates of Cervantes that "the future great artist enters into himself with no less heroism than that of a Montaigne or a Descartes" (*Hacia Cervantes* [Madrid: Taurus, 1957], pp. 262–63); E. C. Riley writes of Cervantes's scruples as "those of the Baconian and Cartesian thinkers of the seventeenth century" (*Cervantes's Theory of the Novel* [Oxford: Clarendon, 1962], p. 162; also p. 223).

cho: "See that you do not deceive me, or seek to cheer my real sadness with false joys" (2.10).

In and despite such doubts, Don Quixote claims (slightly earlier in the narrative) that Dulcinea's force is one of light: "so long as I see her it is all the same to me whether it is over walls or through windows, or chinks or garden grilles. For any ray reaching my eyes from the sun of her beauty will illuminate my understanding and fortify my heart" (2.8). Like the Cartesian narrator for whom God's existence will be proven indubitably in the natural light, Don Quixote apparently expects that he will soon be overwhelmed and persuaded, by her light, of Dulcinea, and that since the enchanters in this instance cannot affect his perceptions, he need make no subsequent corrections. What happens instead (in a scene singled out for comment by Erich Auerbach[13]) is that Sancho introduces—in chivalric phrases—one of the passing peasant girls as the lady Dulcinea while Don Quixote, "his eyes starting out of his head and a puzzled look on his face," can see only peasant girls (2.10). Suddenly put into radical doubt, Dulcinea must be enchanted. *Dulcinea enchanted*: this is as though Descartes's God had somehow turned into the *mal ingénie* and the Cogito itself been abandoned to darkness.

---

[13]*Mimesis*, trans. W. R. Trask (Princeton: Princeton University Press, 1953), pp. 334–58. Auerbach notices how urgent the Dulcinea problem is to the story's economy. Like many commentators, however, he is read by the text he reads: "in our study we are looking for representations of everyday life in which that life is treated seriously, in terms of its human and social problems or even of its tragic complications" (p. 342). Now *Don Quixote* (as Auerbach stresses) offers no such "serious" material, even though it is very "realistic" (pp. 342, 354). This poses difficulties, especially when Auerbach attempts to describe "the whole" (p. 355). Yet rather than questioning his notions of "reality" (and this text, if any, would suggest that he might do so), he argues that the protagonist in his madness has "no point of contact with reality" (p. 344); Auerbach thus inverts quixotic binaries. (For more on his method, see David Carroll, "*Mimesis* Reconsidered," *Diacritics* 5, no. 2 [1975]:5–12.)

Ever *ingenioso*,[14] however, Don Quixote soon seizes upon the discrepancy between what Sancho "sees" and he does not, between *what Sancho thus can say* and he cannot. He infers that thè enchanters in their envy beclouded his eyes but not Sancho's, that they in other words re-troped into a *mala figura* the already well-troped lady, and that what Sancho "correctly" saw, *if not said*—Don Quixote urges—were "eyes like emeralds," not like pearls:

> ". . . Sancho, one thing occurs to me: you described her beauty to me badly. For, if I remember rightly, you said that she had eyes like pearls, and eyes like pearls suit a sea-bream better than a lady. According to my belief, Dulcinea's eyes must be green emeralds, full and large, with twin rainbows to serve them for eyebrows. So take these pearls from her eyes and transfer them to her teeth, for no doubt you got mixed up, Sancho." [2.11]

Don Quixote thus hopes that to rectify or reassemble the linguistic signs of Dulcinea will in some way assist him in his plight.

Plotting moreover to "restore her to her first being [*ser primero*]" (2.11), he is not sure, even so, of what he—as a knight—can do. His thoughts take him "out of himself," *fuera de sí*—the movement by which he gained identity as a knight (2.7) but by which that identity might now be threatened. As Don Quixote is mimed or played with (by readers of part 1, by actors, by "sane" figures), authoring is laid bare as inevitably non-self-referential, a mirroring with an "outside" merely "inside" the mirroring. As against Don Quixote's traditional notions that drama "hold[s] the mirror to us at every step" (2.12), mimetic doubling becomes alarmingly uncontrollable: the knight of the mirrors mirrors a knightly role complete with a detailed claim to have defeated in com-

---

[14]On the term *ingenioso*, see Otis H. Green, "El *Ingenioso* Hidalgo," *Hispanic Review* 25 (1957):175–93, esp. 182–83.

bat all knights of La Mancha, including a certain Don Quixote (2.14). The mirroring is so thorough (with its textual citations and its vaunting of one lady over another) that Don Quixote, instead of saying that the other knight lies, can only explain that the enchanters must have doubled him: "This Don Quixote you speak of . . . is the best friend I have in the world; so much, indeed, that I regard him as I do myself [*que le tengo en lugar de mi misma persona*] and that on the basis of the exact and precise description you have given, I cannot but think that he is the same [*que sea el mismo*] that you conquered" (2.14, tm). The last phrase, made in chary regard for the "other" knight and the enchanters, is a deferential mistake or catechresis—"the same" is not "the same," and the argument Don Quixote goes on to advance (as he might elsewhere promptly notice; 1.48) is inconclusive: "[what] I see with my eyes and touch with my hands cannot possibly be the same being [*no ser possible ser el mismo*], were it not that he had many enemy enchanters, . . . and one could have taken his shape [*figura*] to allow himself to be conquered" (2.14, tm). The repeated "same"—*mismo, mesmo*—almost affiliates Don Quixote with the enchanters he opposes and denies the difference he asserts.

The "I" he employs—and we might again be reminded of Descartes's "I"—functions as a speaker-advocate for "Don Quixote," the latter named and even presented as if someone else: the enchanters "who transformed the figure and person of Dulcinea . . . similarly transformed Don Quixote. . . . [But] here is Don Quixote" (2.14, tm). He insists that another chivalric battle will prove that Don Quixote "is" Don Quixote. Yet just how would another battle (whatever its outcome) be known *not* to be enchanted as well? Don Quixote would like quickly to settle the issue by removing a mirror obstacle—the knight's visor—and (as in the biblical trope) seeing and being seen "face to face" (2.14). When the mirror knight refuses, Don Quixote proposes that just this is what a formal battle will force from him ("I shall see your face, and you shall see that I am not the vanquished Don Quixote you imagine"; 2.14).

Don Quixote triumphs in the ensuing fight, partly because the other knight assumes a naively calculable mirroring ("he went around the field, believing that Don Quixote had done the same"; 2.14, tm). Victorious, Don Quixote sees the knight's face, but only to deny what he sees or to see what "must," by evil enchantment, be yet another doubling: "He saw, our history says, the same face, the same figure, the same aspect, the same physiognomy, the same effigy, the same picture [*pespetiva*] as that of the Bachelor Sanson Carrasco" (2.14, tm). The mirror knight's squire, who turns out to be Sancho's old friend and neighbor, offers to expose (as would Sancho) the "tricks and plots" involved. But Don Quixote is so anxious to limit, if he can, one particular sort of doubling that he ignores all others: his first request is not that the fallen knight clarify his identity but that he praise *and visit* Dulcinea. Only after extracting that specific promise does he then demand that the other, defeated, Don Quixote must have been a mere resemblance, a resemblance that can perhaps be regulated in a face-saving exchange: in return for the knight's belief, Don Quixote will believe that the defeated knight could not be Sanson Carrasco but only his "*figura*" (2.14).

The narrative will unfold the inadequacy of such attempts to control mimetic proliferation. Take the Montesinos cave episode, surrounded with doubts and frequently alluded to in later episodes. The frame story, with projects of bookish genealogies and metamorphic changes, may incite Quixotic desires but with all desires' distortions, as in Ovid's—or the scholar's—"allegories, metaphors and transformations" (2.22). When he descends into the cave, Don Quixote finds that the boundaries of dreaming and living are unclear: he describes a "life," "vision," and "dream" ("*sueño pro-*

fundísimo," "vida y vista") against which the *"contentos d'esta vida"* (which?) pass "like a shadow and dream" (2.22, 23). Don Quixote in the cave must pinch himself to decide whether "I myself was there or some empty and counterfeit phantom" and concludes, less than Cartesianly, that "I was there then just as I am here now" (2.23, tm). Even so (or on that account) the Montesinos *vista* is marked by oneiric displacement and condensation: the knight Durandarte, his heart cut out for his lady, dies yet lives; historically noble ladies "enchanted into different *figuras*" are nonetheless recognizable, including the lady Dulcinea who, as a peasant girl, is there in good company and yet referentially accounted for, though precisely on that account Sancho has strong doubts, and "thought he would . . . die of laughing, . . . knowing as he did the truth about Dulcinea's pretended enchantment, and that he had been her enchanter and the inventor of the story" (2.23).

If the *vista* seems further suspect because of its temporality (Don Quixote's three days juxtaposed to Sancho's hour or so; 2.23), temporality differed-deferred will in the long run presumably also decide or "bring to light" matters of truth or falsity: "the time will come," we are told, when Sancho will believe Don Quixote's truth (2.23). The passing of time vindicates, however, neither Don Quixote nor Sancho: as the duchess tells Sancho, Dulcinea's ostensible enchanter may himself be enchanted:

> ". . . I know that the peasant girl who skipped on to the she-ass really and truly was and is Dulcinea del Toboso, and that it was the good Sancho who was deceived, though he may think he is the deceiver. . . . When least we expect to we shall see her in her proper shape [*en su propia figura*], and then Sancho will be disabused of the delusion under which he labors." [2.33]

The last promise is of course one more ruse among others; the (un-)figuring of figures so as to make them themselves, or proper, will never be definitively accomplished. Indeed Cide Hamete Benengeli, who simultaneously—and marginally—denies, affirms, and is neutral, cannot settle the Montesinos issue even with his certainty about Don Quixote that "at the time of his end and death they say that he retracted [the Montesinos adventure] and he said he had invented it" (2.24, tm). For who is "he"? As the story will show, the "time of end," however authorially useful, is only one among others, and the dying man is not himself—or only himself and not Don Quixote.

III

Such fissures of self may have precedent, we might notice, in the *Metamorphoses* of Ovid, which the humanist scholar (who guides Don Quixote and Sancho to the cave) would domesticate in his Spanish Ovid (2,22, 24). Ovidian metamorphoses occur as terrifying loosenings into hierarchically inferior (supposedly dominated, nonhuman) forms of (non-) self. The *Metamorphoses* moves as free-play, interrogating a number of Western norms—of rulership or fatherhood (Phaëthon, Daedalus), of "auto-affection" (Narcissus and Echo), of mimetic and "unified" narrative (fantastic myths framed by a nominal historical scheme but in a sequence that is fluctuating or decentered).[15] Selves radically altered force the question, How are our bodies—and our genealogies or names—ours? No answer is given by "philosophy" (recall Pythagoras, *Metamorphoses*, XV) but Ovid's poetry shows anatomically impeded voice: a newly changed Io tried

---

[15]On Ovid's non-Augustan attitudes, see Brooks Otis, *Ovid as an Epic Poet* (Cambridge: Cambridge University Press, 1966), pp. 4–22; Karl Galinsky, *Ovid's Metamorphoses* (Berkeley: University of California Press, 1975), pp. 145, 185–265. See also Charles Altieri, "Ovid and the New Mythologists," *Novel* 7, no. 1 (1973):31–40, and John Brenkman, "Narcissus in the Text," *Georgia Review* 30 (1976):293–327. Altieri emphasizes more than Brenkman how Ovidian free-play is at once a challenge to conventional poetics and a sign of authorial mastery.

to complain, but "sheer bellowing came out of her mouth, and frightened by her own voice [*propria voce*], . . . she fled from herself" (I.635 ff.).[16]

The concept of self, here as elsewhere, is questioned. In the Narcissus-Echo story (with analogues in the Cervantine ass-brayers), Tiresias—whose very appearance recalls Oedipus—predicts that Narcissus will live to a ripe old age "if he does not know himself" (III.348). Since Narcissus dies young and Tiresias is then widely acclaimed, self-knowledge is presumably achieved even as the very concept may come under critical scrutiny (Narcissus loves a reflection). Narcissus spellbound is a marble statue (*signum*; III.419), but the auto-affective illusion is dispersed when the water ripples and when his "same" voice, with Echo's supplementation, can only be different—it is neither his nor hers. At first, Echo echoes Narcissus:

> By chance Narcissus
> Lost track of his companions, started calling
> "Is anybody here?" and "Here!" said Echo.
> He looked around in wonderment, called louder
> "Come to me!" "Come to me!" came back the answer.
>
> [III.379–84]

Later he in turn, looking in the water, reiterates the situation, though with himself:

> You promise,
> I think, some hope with a look of more than friendship.
> You reach out arms when I do, and your smile
> Follows my smiling; I have seen your tears
> When I was tearful. . . .
>
> [III.457–60]

Narcissus concedes that loverlike he may be in error, that he knows who he is and that what he loves is his image

---

[16]*Metamorphoseon*, ed. D. E. Bosselaar (Leiden: Brill, 1959), my translation. The verse translations below are from Ovid, *Metamorphoses*, trans. Rolfe Humphries (Bloomington: Indiana University Press, 1955).

(III.463–67). But this only makes him more concerned than ever with "his" self-(un-)making mirrored-fractured reflection: the surface of the water is disturbed by tears (III.477–84). Narcissus's self-knowledge, if it is that, is necessarily and only *like him*.

Although Ovid thereby clarifies or subsumes the "*vox auguris*" of Tiresias (which was "*vana*" before the story's unfolding), he also playfully tests—demystifies but also reconfirms—his own stance as poetic *auctor*. Mythic happenings occasion a doubt that is surprise: Deucalion and Pyrrha, perplexed at an oracle's dark words, are forced into mythic readings that are immediately vindicated in the poem's "now," which must be (amusingly) a venerable not-now (I.400). Daedalus, again, made a complexly confusing maze in which he was almost caught, then "set his mind to unknown arts, changing nature" (VIII.188). The words hark back to Ovid's opening lines of the *perpetuum carmen*, but not quite; Daedalus builds wings to fly, as if making rather than telling a metamorphosis, and he cannot guide his deviating Icarus, who cries "Father!" just when the word no longer can apply.

If Ovidian metamorphoses are contained by assumptions of cosmic continuity or poetic power,[17] Cervantine enchantments seem illimitable in their effects on any "author." Notice the unknowability of the enemy enchanters' capacities, against which the knight's most frequent belief is that the en-

---

[17]The assumptions are at work in the Orpheus story. This story has been taken to suggest, for writers like Maurice Blanchot and Roland Barthes, a poetics of indirection and negation: Orpheus's song is of an absent Eurydice who only "is" in the song in which she is not (Blanchot, *L'éspace littéraire* [Paris: Gallimard, 1955], pp. 227–34; Barthes, *Critical Essays*, trans. R. Howard [Evanston: Northwestern University Press, 1972], pp. 156–57). Ovid also celebrates, however, the power over natural forces (X.144) of the singer whose singing merges with his own (Orpheus performs most of book X in strict stylistic continuity). The maenads seek and dismember "Orpheus singing with his lyre," his *nervis*—sinew, gut, nerve—his song's strength (XI.5); but the head and lyre, even so, sing on. An Orphic poetics—song in persuasive power over the world—can never quite die, or so Ovid asserts (poetically, of himself as poet) in the concluding lines of the *Metamorphoses*.

chanters can change appearances only: enchantments, he tells Sancho, "change all things from their natural state [*ser natural*], [but] I do not mean that they really change one thing [*ser*] into another, but that they appear to, as we were shown in Dulcinea's enchantment" (2.29, tm). The story's "closure," however, involves the incomplete subversion or deconstruction of the essence/appearance binary, or of "Dulcinea" and then "Don Quixote" as signs. Recall the vacillation between Don Quixote as his own light (2.32, 36) and Don Quixote as dependent on the Dulcinean light, which somehow, impossibly, is darkened. When the duke and duchess ask for a description of Dulcinea, Don Quixote responds wistfully that his idea of her has been erased (*borrado*) by her recent misfortune and that the enchanters will deprive him "of the eyes with which he looks [*con que mira*] and of the sun which gives him light," persecuting him into the "deep abyss of oblivion" (2.32, tm). The question, indeed, throughout part 2 is whether Dulcinea has been metamorphosed merely in appearance (as signifier) while remaining untouched in essence (as signified) or—though this is not quite equivalent—whether her "enchantment" can be reversed, that is, whether she can be reconstructed.

Don Quixote and Sancho, having "seen" Dulcinea (though differently in form), can vouch for her existence, and Don Quixote can yearn for her in her *ser original*, a possibility unlikely to have arisen had she not been enchanted out of it. It is now no longer enough (though Don Quixote says otherwise) for her to be "imprinted in . . . my heart and in my innermost entrails" (2.48). For if Dulcinea is out of order, Don Quixote may be out of order as well.

A balancing or supplementation defers his problems; just when Don Quixote begins to believe that (without Dulcinea) he is vulnerable as a knight, his narrative paradigm seems to be nearing fulfillment. Earlier he had described, as we noted, the pattern:

A knight, . . . when he arrives at the court of some great monarch, will already be known by his deeds. Then as soon as the boys see him ride through the city gates, they will all follow him and surround him and shout: "Here is the Knight of the Sun!—or of the Serpent . . ." [1.21, tm]

Now as Don Quixote himself enters the ducal palace:

In an instant all the galleries of the court were crowded with the Duke and Duchess's men and women servants, crying loudly: "Welcome to the flower and cream of knights errant." . . . And this was the first time that he was positively certain of being a true and no imaginary knight errant, since he found himself treated just as he had read these knights were treated in past ages. [2.31]

The burdens and doubts of proving himself a knight may seem to be overcome. Yet during his visit, on the contrary, he worries about decorum and is incessantly joked with.[18] The dukes devise a method that might restore "Dulcinea," but as Don Quixote may be half aware, the assumption that he will be restored if Dulcinea is restored is ominously close to (or poorly disguises) the negative converse that because he had been less than a knight, she is less than his lady. Such reversibilities seem uncontainable, and the enchanters seem less likely than ever to be identified.

IV

The widening hiatus, we are saying, between Don Quixote and his knighthood occurs as a dismantling of chivalric signs. When Don Quixote on a roadway challengingly proclaims Dulcinea's greatness, he is trampled by a herd of bulls, and the only relation between the two actions is mere juxtaposition, not causality (2.58). Don Quixote himself

[18]On the shifts between part 1 and part 2, see Ruth S. El Saffar, *Novel to Romance* (Baltimore: Johns Hopkins University Press, 1974), pp. 1–10.

makes rhetorical use of the contrast: "Printed in histories, famous in arms, . . . [yet] trampled, kicked and pounded by the feet of unclean and filthy animals" (2.59). In and despite the contrast, there may be no difference, and this is one among other instances, undecisive in themselves but cumulative in effect, in which dismantling takes place: (1) disputes about Montesinos leading to Don Quixote's whispered suggestion of a cognitive exchange ("if you want me to believe what you saw, . . . I wish you to believe what I saw"; 2.41), (2) battles occurring in silence, nonheroically, often nonpublicly, "without any sound of trumpet or warlike instrument" (2.64, 48), (3) Don Quixote and Sancho, defeated, being surrounded by silent and silencing captors who fail to address them except with abusive, monstrous epithets (2.68), (4) Don Quixote naming the rhetorical figures he uses ("so that you may believe in this exaggeration of mine, know that I am Don Quixote"; 2.58, tm; also 73).

Other instances, too, merit some scrutiny. Don Quixote claims as a Christian to reject omens; those who believe them, he says, act as if nature were obliged to give signs of approaching disasters by unimportant things (2.43; cf. 2.22). Yet when, after Sancho's whipping (which is supposed to "disenchant" Dulcinea and restore her to her original form), Don Quixote fails to see his lady, he catches at the words of some local boys at play and cries out *malum signum!* (2.73). Sancho, rejecting omens, shows the words to be entirely irrelevant to Don Quixote's plight: he breaks apart the sign he had just seemed, by his whipping, almost to reconstitute; not only does Dulcinea fail to appear, but *there are not even signs of her nonappearance.* We need not be tempted to thematize the Dulcinea dismantling, however, by linking it to narrative movements from Don Quixote to Alonso Quixano, from madness to sanity and death or still less from "false" (chivalric) to "true" (Cervantine) writing. The author-enchanters in their increasing absence-silence may work as powerfully as ever and, in a dizzying production/nonproduction aporia, can never be simply designated as falsifiers, forgers, madmen, or even poor writers. Characters offer stories about themselves, but the stories are often disguised or incomplete (1.22), and the text suggests repeatedly that there can be no secure authorial signature. If a story is likely to require some—but not too many—referentially "correct" details, when and for whom do those details become irrelevant or deleterious to the much-mentioned "truth of the story"? Traditional "truth"—bounded, single, steady—is displaced by a far less decidable "truth." Thus in and despite endless evaluations of "authorial" doings, the doings can never be normatively systematized—parodic oppositions are repetitions and paradoxes[19] that the story's progress fails to synthesize. This is apparent both in relations between Don Quixote and Sancho and in relations between Cide Hamete, "Cervantes," and Avellaneda.

The oscillating Don Quixote–Sancho relation, to begin with, cannot be fixed as dominance, opposition, equality, or subversion. Sancho makes efforts to demystify Don Quixote's notions, but such efforts provide Don Quixote with occasions for counterdemystifications and "authoritative" explanations ("[Sancho,] you know very little of this subject of adventures"; 1.8,18). When Sancho notifies an encaged Don Quixote that his captors are the local barber and priest, Don Quixote warns him that the enchanters "assumed the likeness of our friends . . . to put you into a maze of conjectures" (1.48). When Sancho nonetheless persists that his master cannot be enchanted, Don Quixote responds magisterially that enchanters may be deceptive even in their tactics of enchantment, that every appearance against enchantment may merely be an indication of it. Although Sancho later thinks (in presenting the peasant girls) that he can

[19]On parody as paradox, see Dorothy van Ghent, *The English Novel: Form and Function* (New York: Rinehart, 1953), pp. 9–19.

make use of such ambiguities, his effort—which sets in motion Dulcinea's deconstruction—is itself ambiguous in its "success." If his master thereafter raises Sancho to governship, Sancho, though able sagely to rule, soon rejects the governship. Yet does he reject it as hierarchy or pseudohierarchy? "Let me . . . rise again from this present death" could have been uttered at more or less this point (2.53) by either Don Quixote or Sancho, both of whom distance themselves from one another precisely at the moment that they become most alike.

Similarly with authorial issues: Avellaneda had written an alternative second part for *Don Quixote*, but to what extent can the Cervantine author claim that his text, of all texts, is more "genuine" or "original" or "true"? Any such claim would be quixotic. Indeed, where the author (enchanter) allows Avellaneda the potency to engender "another" Don Quixote and Sancho Panza, it is mostly Don Quixote who criticizes the "other" author's bad writing and who makes Don Álvaro swear that only the "present" Don Quixote and Sancho Panza are real (2.72). To what extent, we might wonder then, is the parody against Avellaneda's (or Cide Hamete's) offspring *not* also against that of "Cervantes"? Often, to be sure, a parodic gap is obvious, as in the hyperbolic praise of Cide Hamete, who "leaves nothing, however minute it may be, which he does not bring to light" (2.40, tm). But such gaps prepare for others more equivocal: the quixotic sign's undoing partially overlaps with (and is disguised by) logocentric nostalgias of "end."

In many ways *Don Quixote* is endless;[20] "victories" alternate with "defeats," which can in turn be perpetually "explained." It is the fictional author, we might notice, who gives signals of closure: "'human life speeds to its end faster than the wind, without hope of renewal, except in that other

[20]See Robert M. Adams, *Strains of Discord* (Ithaca: Cornell University Press, 1958), p. 81.

life. . . .' So says Cide Hamete, the Mohammedan philosopher; . . . [who] alludes only to the swiftness with which Sancho's government ended" (2.53). Here topoi of closure are immediately deflated—they are conventional, mawkish, possibly insincere. And the elegy preceding Don Quixote's death, although not explicitly cited as Cide Hamete's, is suspect by resemblance: "Since human things are not eternal, moving in decline from their beginnings [*principios*] until they reach their final end, especially the lives of men, . . . Don Quixote's end came when he least expected it" (2.74, tm). Steady "decline" endows the movement with a predictability also being denied, as if two topoi, since they are both conventional (death is inevitable, death is surprising), must both be employed: the writer is drawing on his stock and performing as best he can, after all, his authorial duty.

Similar topoi (presumably comforting in their familiarity) are similarly banal: a restored Alonso Quixano rejects his earlier self, commenting that "there are no birds this year in last year's nest"; the bulls who trample Don Quixote take no more notice of his threats "than of yesteryear's clouds" and, by the same expression, omens are irrelevant to his plight (2.74, 58, 73). These topoi of time as culmination—and domesticated futility—occur at moments (we noted earlier) of deconstruction, and their suggestions of narrative integration poorly disguise the differences that make them possible. With no Ovidian presumptions to contain metamorphoses, the Cervantine author ends by guardedly citing the author-*persona* who not only believes that he will put a stop, with Don Quixote's death, to further "falsifiers" like Avellaneda but believes that he has realized the project's *mira*: he "enjoys entirely the fruit of his writing" (2.74, tm). For an "other" author—call him, if you will, Cervantes—any such *mira* must look like some glittering mirror, a mirage.

5

Changeling Fathering:
Tristram Shandy

The well-shaped changeling is a man, has a rational soul,
though it appear not: this is past doubt, say you: make the
ears a little longer, and more pointed, and the nose a little
flatter than ordinary, and then you begin to boggle; make
the face yet narrower, flatter, . . . then presently it is a
monster. . . . Where now (I ask) shall be the just measure;
which the utmost bounds of that shape, that carries with it
a rational soul? For, since there have been human foetuses
produced, [that] may have several degrees of mixture of
the likeness of a man or a brute;—I would gladly know
what are those precise lineaments, which, according to this
hypothesis, are or are not capable of a rational soul to be
joined to them. What sort of outside is the certain sign that
there is or is not such an inhabitant within? For till that be
done, we talk at random of *man*. . . .
—John Locke, *An Essay Concerning Human Understanding*

Many literary critics assume that literature, almost to
the extent that it is worthwhile, cherishes and conveys humanistic themes.[1] A good deal would seem to be at stake,
then, in the entire recent movement that puts humanism
into question—mildly at first in the texts of Jean-Paul Sartre
but with increasing severity in those of Martin Heidegger,
Michel Foucault, and Jacques Derrida. The questioning of
humanism, however, despite its recent prominence, may

[1]See for instance the references to Curtius and Auerbach above, Chap. 1,
n. 54.

have been anticipated in some ways from "within" the tradition, anticipated not in controversies between the Church and Galileo or between Renaissance modernists and classicists but more subtly, yet radically, in literary texts whose rhetorical strategies take apart representations, particularly of "the human." This operation often occurs in satires, and the text considered in this chapter—Laurence Sterne's *The Life and Opinions of Tristram Shandy, Gentleman*—questions "the human" rather oddly, by means of an embedded metaphorics of misbirth or monstrosity.

Such a questioning overlaps with a Derridean statement cited earlier:

> There is a kind of question . . . whose *conception, formation, gestation* and *labor* we are only catching a glimpse of today. I say these words with eyes turned [*tournés*], to be sure, toward . . . those who . . . turn them away [*les détournent*] before the still unnamable that announces itself, and cannot do so . . . except under the species of a nonspecies, in the formless, mute, infant, and terrifying form of monstrosity.[2]

Any "representation" of monstrosity is likely to be a contradiction. And commentators on *Tristram Shandy* may have turned away their eyes from certain aspects of John Locke's *Essay Concerning Human Understanding*, whose intertextual connections with *Tristram Shandy* they have been otherwise adept at seeing. They may have turned away their eyes, too, from a Sternean reading of Locke on Sir Robert Filmer's *De Patriarcha* or of Dr. John Burton's *Letter to Dr. Smellie* and his "Account of a Monstrous Child." These texts, with their undeniable implications for the question of the properly human, are relatable to the problem of humanism remarked in the preface of this book and, more specifically, to certain recent texts.

---

[2]Jacques Derrida, "Structure, Sign and Play in the Discourse of the Human Sciences," in *Writing and Difference*, trans. A. Bass (Chicago: University of Chicago Press, 1978), p. 293; *L'écriture et la différence* (Paris: Seuil, 1967), p. 428 (Derrida's emphasis).

In his "Letter on Humanism," for instance, Heidegger speaks of a threat "to the essence of humanity."[3] Although "essence" is meant in a special way, Heidegger's setting aside of humanism is curiously traditional: humanism neglects "the proper dignity of man" and "does not set the *humanitas* of man high enough."[4] The terms are presumably to be held at some distance from what is being said, yet there can be no foolproof insurance that the distance can be kept, that is, that the discourse will not become entangled in the tradition that it tries to oppose. The danger seems to be in dumbness, in not questioning: Derrida writes (in "The Ends of Man") that "despite a supposed neutralization of metaphysical presuppositions, it is necessary to recognize that the unity of man is in itself never seriously interrogated"; in Sartre, he continues, there is a facile gliding from the "we" of philosophic discourse to the "we" of all humans.[5] Similarly, "What is there then of this *we* in the text of Heidegger?" With a sly graciousness, Derrida's very next sentence shows a "we": "This question is the most difficult and we can do no more than to broach it [*amorcer*: to allure, to decoy]."[6] Indeed if the question is so difficult, we might wonder how and to what extent yet another interrogation will be less of a decoy.

Derrida's tactic is to underline in Heidegger's text the notion of proximity (presence to self and to Being) and the metaphors of guardianship, household and voice, all of which allow Heidegger the "subtle" and "equivocal" gesture of *relève* or recuperation of humanism.[7] Such an analysis,

[3]*Basic Writings*, ed. David F. Krell (New York: Harper & Row, 1977), p. 198.

[4]*Ibid.*, p. 210.

[5]*Marges de la philosophie* (Paris: Minuit, 1972), pp. 136–37. Some recent reflections by Derrida and others on the question of humanism can be found in *Les fins de l'homme: A partir du travail de Jacques Derrida*, ed. P. Lacoue-Labarthe and J.-L. Nancy (Paris: Galilée, 1981).

[6]*Marges*, p. 147.

[7]*Ibid.*, pp. 148, 151, 156.

which might be called a deconstruction, offers not merely a
marking out of metaphors, but—here resides its power—a
strong implication that these metaphors have a rhetorical
function, that is, that they are being used upon or against,
after all, "us." Since rhetorical analysis is never innocent or
neutral but always involved in plays of power, the gesture
that recuperates humanism can never be entirely avoided.[8]
To be rhetorically effective, the "we" of Derrida, even if offered ironically, must be read as to some extent proximate
or proper, albeit with variably equivocal re-plays of the
"end" of man as *telos*/death. This is not to deny Derridean
radicality, but to stress its questioning—which may be all too
implicit—of deconstruction and recuperation as binary oppositions.

Here assistance may come from *Tristram Shandy*, which
constantly rehearses the *telos*/death problem and which cannot be called simply an undoing or a recuperation but only
some strange breed of both. There can thus be no quick
route to humanism in the Shandean text, and perhaps no
route at all.

I

To clarify what is at issue, recall the usual motifs of Western humanism—articulateness, education, exploration, cre-
ativity, utopianism—or more specifically, the thematic messages that many critics claim to find in the texts they value
most highly, messages having to do with the complexity of

[8]This situation is apparent in Foucault: "my aim was to analyze [the his-
tory of thought] in the discontinuity that no teleology would reduce in ad-
vance"; but the phrase "my aim" is problematic, and Foucault admits to
some embarrassment when asked, "What then is the title of your discourse?
Where does it come from and from where does it derive its right to speak?"
(*The Archaeology of Knowledge*, trans. A. M. Smith [New York: Harper &
Row, 1972], pp. 203, 205). See also Hubert Dreyfus and Paul Rabinow,
Michel Foucault: Beyond Structuralism and Hermeneutics (Chicago: University of
Chicago Press, 1982), esp. pp. 95–109.

human selves in temporary or resolvable disharmony with some sort of community of widely shared values. My contention will be that the Shandean text, like the Shandys in their deformities, is difficult to reconcile with such critical norms, and that the very process by which we read humanistic messages must be subjected to painstaking scrutiny.

There are, to be sure, commentators such as F. R. Leavis who would simply exclude *Tristram Shandy* from the so-called Great Tradition.[9] There are others, however, who would positively assess the text, but only by making it fit their various schemes. Consider for instance the sorts of recuperation, about which we might be somewhat dubious, marking a number of recent readings. Melvyn New argues that *Tristram Shandy* is a satire with a "norm" to be measured in Yorick as against Tristram, while Helene Moglen, who postulates that Locke provided Sterne with an "underlying rational structure," is concerned to prove that the text is novelistic.[10] Similarly, if perhaps more astonishingly, James Swearingen would align "Tristram's method" with Edmund Husserl's "foundations of a general phenomenology,"[11] and the text becomes valuable as an ostensible confirmation of the Husserlian privileging of presence: "Tristram Shandy's reflections lead through a combined archeology and teleology of the self to a clear understanding of the structure . . . of his own being."[12] Conveniently ignorant of (or turning his eyes from) the Derridean reading of Husserl's theory of signs,[13] Swearingen urges that "Tristram's whole enterprise" is a "hermeneutics" that rectifies—or in other terms, which I shall question, does justice to—"serious misinterpretation"

[9]*The Great Tradition* (London: Chatto & Windus, 1948), p. 2.
[10]Melvyn New, *Laurence Sterne as Satirist* (Gainesville: University of Florida Press, 1969), pp. 76–81; Helene Moglen, *The Philosophical Irony of Laurence Sterne* (Gainesville: University of Florida Press, 1975), pp. 16, 27.
[11]*Reflexivity in "Tristram Shandy"* (New Haven: Yale University Press, 1977), p. 55.
[12]*Ibid.*, p. 3.
[13]*Speech and Phenomena*, trans. D. Allison (Evanston: Northwestern University Press, 1973).

of his family and tradition, while providing a reassuring "intimacy of the autobiographical voice," a "profound ontological intimacy."[14]

Any such intimacy, however, is ambiguous, and a reading like Swearingen's must ignore the ungrounded figurality in which the responses of an imaginarily "present" audience become Tristram's rhetoric about rhetorical effects. What one might be tempted to take as Sterne's message or method may be, monstrously, little more than a rhetorical gesture or (here is the complication) even less, since in *Tristram Shandy* "rhetoric" as either trope or persuasion is endlessly deconstructed.[15] Tristram toys with imagined communication but is more interested in obstacles or means than in "results" (which turn out repeatedly to be new obstacles and means); as persuasion, Tristram's helter-skelter opinions and didacticism (the pointed hands, the diagrams, the moral lessons) are addressed to "his" audience, and that transaction itself becomes a show for narratees who are not necessarily "us" as readers.

Commentators have recognized this situation, though mostly to the extent that they avoid the concept of "rhetoric" in any simple sense: the text's specification of figures cannot be construed, as Graham Petrie, for instance, contends, as Sterne's effort "to explain to the reader his reasons for constructing his novel" as he does.[16] Readers, after all, may be eager to make themselves party to a debate about some "central point of view" in (or in opposition to) the text's rhetorical effects. But debate is only one sort of play among others; as Richard Lanham remarks, "those who seek—or deny—in *Tristram Shandy* a high seriousness, presume the novel a de-

---

[14]Swearingen, *Reflexivity in "Tristram Shandy,"* pp. 6, 4, 82.

[15]Paul de Man's remarks on Nietzsche also apply to *Tristram Shandy*: "Considered as persuasion, rhetoric is performative but when considered as a system of tropes, it deconstructs its own performance" (*Allegories of Reading* [New Haven: Yale University Press, 1979], p. 131).

[16]"Rhetoric as Fictional Technique in *Tristram Shandy,*" *Philological Quarterly* 48 (1969):480.

bate [rather than] a game, . . . [that is, than] a continuing
contest with, by its nature, only intermediate results"; the
problem is that *Tristram Shandy* seems to play at being serious—it "denies us a single point of view . . . [as it] continually
alerts us for the need for one."[17] Thus, in part, its uneasy
relationship with Lockean texts: Tristram, with a leering
grin at Locke's project to minimize linguistic "abuse" by min-
imizing tropes, elaborates a rhetoric about rhetoric in which
figures, as John Traugott observes, "are not allowed to serve
in their own significations."[18] We may question whether this
is rhetoric as familiarly understood—let us call it, instead,
rhetoricity—or even whether such figures can be reinstated,
as Traugott goes on to suggest, as a "symbol" or "part" of
the "thinking process," since "thinking" in *Tristram Shandy*
does not (or does not only) move according to a logic of binary oppositions.

The assumption of such a logic, however, is the basis for
many readings. Consider for instance William J. Farrell's
pointing to how "Tristram will mistake an unconscious turn
in an ordinary conversation for some premeditated figure of
speech": Tristram almost credits Uncle Toby, interrupted in
a comment about his sister, with an aposiopesis, and credits
Mr. Shandy with being a "natural" orator, although the latter uses—indeed exaggeratedly—the artifices of the rhetorical handbooks.[19] Does Tristram, however, make his mistakes mistakenly? Farrell assumes that "nature" is taken for
"art" and "art" for "nature," that Tristram—who ought to

[17]*"Tristram Shandy": The Games of Pleasure* (Berkeley: University of California Press, 1973), pp. 45, 98.

[18]*Tristram Shandy's World: Sterne's Philosophical Rhetoric* (Berkeley: University of California Press, 1954), p. 122. Similarly, Viktor Shklovsky notes that
the Shandean text is atypically typical: the writer "lays bare" the literary de-
vice; "form is presented simply as such, without any kind of motivation" ("A
Parodying Novel: *Tristram Shandy*," in Lee T. Lemon and Marion J. Reis,
eds., *Russian Formalist Criticism* [Lincoln: University of Nebraska Press,
1965], pp. 27, 57). On Locke's anti-tropological project, see Paul de Man,
"The Epistemology of Metaphor," *Critical Inquiry*, 4 (1978):13–22.

[19]"Nature versus Art as a Comic Pattern in *Tristram Shandy*," *ELH* 30
(1963):16–19.

know which is which—is thus being mocked ("the foolish narrator imposes art where there really is no art") and finally that Sterne, who presumably knows which is which, retains proper differences ("It would be a serious mistake to confuse Tristram's obvious and inept techniques with Sterne's . . . art").[20] What this refuses to allow is that Tristram is not merely inverting or mistaking binaries but is in effect calling them into question; one particular word, indeed, Farrell places in quotation marks: "The actual or 'natural' situation : . . completely contradicts Tristram's rhetorical interpretation of it and makes it sound foolish."[21] Why is there an implicit equation of actual rather than "actual" with "natural"? And is "sounding foolish" actual or "actual," natural or "natural"?

Such questions are pertinent, since in *Tristram Shandy* the words "nature" and "natural" are given careful attention: they are Lockean favorites, and likely to appear whenever questions of being "human" or a "man" are raised. What the learned doctors call the *"Non-Naturals,"* Tristram notices, are "the most natural actions of a man's life" (1.23),[22] while Mrs. Shandy's questions at his begetting came from ideas that have "no connection in nature" (1.4). The last phrase is of course from Locke, where "nature" (like "natural law") is taken for granted and privileged: "By *real ideas*, I mean such as have a foundation in nature; such as have a conformity with the real being and existence of things, or with their archetypes. *Fantastical* or *chimerical*, I call such as have no foundation in nature."[23] The most reliable ideas are "simple" ones that presumably "intimate some real existence," though

---

[20]*Ibid.*, pp. 29, 34.

[21]*Ibid.*, p. 18.

[22]References to *Tristram Shandy* are by book and chapter in the edition of James A. Work (New York: Odyssey, 1940). The "Non-Naturals" (such as air, meat, drink, excretion, sleep, and movement) designated, at the time, what was not part of the body yet vital to it. Dr. John Burton, we might note, composed *A Treatise of the Non-Naturals* (York: Staples, 1738).

[23]*An Essay Concerning Human Understanding*, ed. Alexander C. Fraser (1894; repr. New York: Dover, 1959) [hereafter, *Essay*], 2.30.1.

in their very simplicity they cannot be defined and so may be "the occasion of great wrangling and obscurity."[24] "Nature," however "simple" an idea, is held to intimate some "real existence," but that intimation—as Locke repeatedly notes—is vexed.

This being so, we might wonder about Locke's pedagogic program for parents "diligently to watch, and carefully to prevent the undue connexion of ideas in the minds of young people."[25] Granted the lifelong dangers that could ensue from the "wrong connexion of ideas" in a young child (and Tristram cites the passage; 1.1), at just what point or by what standard is the connection no longer "in nature" but "undue" or "wrong"? How can connections be known "to set us awry in our actions, as well moral as natural, passions, reasonings and notions,"[26] particularly if the overseeing parents themselves may have long since been "set awry"? In *Tristram Shandy* a damaging "combination of ideas, not allied by nature"[27] seems always already to have occurred: Tristram places himself as if "diligently to watch" his parents' "undue connexion," and little can be done "carefully to prevent" what follows. The "animal spirits" that, Tristram says, "were scattered and dispersed . . . whose business it was to have escorted and gone hand-in-hand with the HOMUNCULUS" (1.2) are, by Locke's account, indeterminately "natural": in their "trains of motions" they may be the "natural cause" of unnaturally connected ideas or of feelings that "produce as regular effects as if they were natural." This surely may lead to confusion, and Locke adds that there are other feelings that "are truly natural, depend on our original constitution, and are born with us."[28] Can any connections be "natural," however, if (as with Tristram) our "original constitution" is already affected by scattering?

[24]*Ibid.*, 3.4.2, 3.4.4.
[25]*Ibid.*, 2.33.8.
[26]*Ibid.*, 22.33.9.
[27]*Ibid.*, 2.33.6; *Tristram Shandy*, 1.4.
[28]*Essay*, 2.33.7.

The animal spirits' task "was to have" guided the homunculus, but (considering the tense) they might not have done so. If not, there is cause for alarm: "What if any accident had befallen him in his way alone?" (1.2). An accident in *Tristram Shandy* is extremely likely, and although the "minutest philosophers" may have vouched for the homunculus as "our fellow creature," he may have been weakened in ways "which no skill of the physician or the philosopher" could rectify (1.2). Thus his very humanity—of which Tristram, citing authorities, makes a painstaking defense—might have been put irreversibly into question. Recall the defense: the homunculus is "engender'd in the same course of nature" and possesses "the same" physical attributes as humans—"skin, hair, fat, flesh, veins, arteries, ligaments, nerves, cartilages" (1.2). Since these attributes are shared with animals, though, they are not definitively "human"; again, what of the cases (so fascinating to Locke) in which "nature" apparently differs from itself and produces monstrous children? If with homunculi, as with ideas, the animal spirits may misgovern, are the resulting children "chimerical" who are born with attributes "never united in nature"? If so, at what point? At what point does "nature" cease to be "natural" or begin (or cease) to be "human"? Locke's procedure is characteristic: at what point do attributes (like acorns or apples in the "state of nature") become a man's legitimate "property"? "When he digested? Or when he eat? Or when he boiled? Or when he brought them home? Or when he pickt them up?"[29] The series of rhetorical questions, like other Lockean series (as in my epigraph) is often more powerful than the proper answer that supposedly contains it. In relation to what "foundations" can deviations be established as such?

With regard to being "human," this question is problem-

[29]*Second Treatise of Government*, chap. 5, # 28, in Peter Laslett, ed., *Two Treatises of Government* (1960; repr. New York: New American Library, 1963).

atic, since at any point in the process of birth, a deviation of
or from (that is, supplementing) "nature" may occur. Consider the latter instance: the midwife assists in the process of
labor and is often assisted with tools. The man midwife is
more supplementary than the woman midwife; Walter
Shandy favors a man midwife on the basis of arguments similar, no doubt, to those Dr. John Burton advances in his
lengthy (250-page) *Letter to William Smellie, M.D.*: a man is
not only likely to be physically stronger but is more likely to
use the latest obstetrical instruments.[30] Since among men
midwives there apparently may arise disputes, however,
these virtues may seem questionable, and not surprisingly
Burton from the very outset establishes the polemical issue
as a rather broad one: what Smellie has done is "to con-
found all Nature———all Distinction of Sex———To make
Animals Vegetables, and one and the same Author two different Persons; and neither Character agree with the true
one."[31] Presumably Burton's own authorship is the more secure in that it recognizes and decries such monstrous confu-
sions. Yet his long cumulative sentence (as Tristram does not
fail to notice; 2.19) builds up to a rather strange climax:
Smellie's worst error was to have mistaken the drawing of a
petrified child for an author or, as Burton puts it, to have
"converted *Lithopaedii Senonensis Icon*, . . . an inanimate pet-
refied Substance, into an Author."[32]

Surely an author deserves more respect than this, Burton
implies, and indeed his own position as author and physician, as against Smellie's, is constantly at issue—apparently
far more so than the actual obstetrical techniques under discussion or than the condition of the infant being extracted.
That infant is given indeed virtually no attention, and often

[30]John Burton, M.D., *A Letter to William Smellie, M.D.* (London: Owen,
1753), pp. 119, 129.
[31]*Ibid.*, p. 1.
[32]*Ibid.*

we are unclear as to whether it is dead or alive. Dr. Burton's obstetrical instruments seem to work best on a dead child, or else will seriously maim the child's intelligence. For repeatedly the most troublesome anatomical part is the head, and some way must be found to move it out of the pelvis: "if the Child's Head be so large, as not to be extracted whole, it must first be opened to let out Part of its Contents."[33] Burton cites approvingly the obstetrician La Motte, who recommends that "the common Scissars may be thrust into the Head, opening them wide to enlarge the Orifice."[34] La Motte than "evacuated the Brain" with his fingers, later using the forceps, "fixing one Branch in the inside of the Skull and the other on the Outside," thereby extracting the (brainless) child.[35]

Dr. Burton occasionally ponders damage that may be done, but he always views the child under the aspect of an obstacle to be removed or an object like other objects, though somewhat more fragile: "The Injuries that may happen to a Child by turning it, may arise from breaking its Limbs,———from compressing the Head too much, and from a Dislocation or Separation of the Vertebrae of the Neck."[36] Such injuries are likely when the child is firmly lodged, that is, when neither the pressure of the laboring mother (whereby "the Brain is forced towards the Cerebellum") nor of the forceps (which "must add considerably to the Compressure") are sufficient.[37] In such instances a man midwife is called for, and Dr. Burton recounts, with considerable professional pride, a rather difficult case:

> . . . The head stuck at the Brim of the Pelvis, altho' I turned the Chin to one Side of that Opening, and tried to make it ad-

[33]*Ibid.*, p. 129.
[34]*Ibid.*, p. 54.
[35]*Ibid.*, p. 55.
[36]*Ibid.*, p. 120.
[37]*Ibid.*, p. 123.

vance, sometimes with a Finger in the Child's Mouth, and sometimes by pushing up the Chin, to get the broadest part of the Cranium to one Side of the Pelvis, at the same time pulling at the Shoulders, with no small force, but all in vain. This Method I repeated two or three times with no better Success, wherefore I exerted my utmost Strength, when I found the Vertebrae of the Neck began to separate from those of the Back; and by continuing the same means, the Head and Body were soon parted: I . . . introduced my Extractor, and immediately extracted the Head.[38]

The triumph in this proceeding is presumably to have spared the mother. But what of the child? If in this instance the child dies or is dead, we can imagine instances of its being born, alive perhaps, but with a crushed skull or "evacuated" brain, that is, as an aberration whose monstrosity occurs in a process that is never simply natural. No wonder Tristram Shandy, if making a case for his humanity, takes notice of the circumstances of his so-called delivery. The man midwife Dr. Slop, like Dr. Burton, seems somewhat too ready to "break the Fabric of the Brain"[39] and the Shandys, father and son, fret repeatedly about a "network" or "intellectual web" in the cerebellum, a system (of understanding, of language, of communication) that at some point may have been irremediably undone (2.19, 4.19, 7.2).

This itself, however, may both disguise and heighten yet another possibility, namely, that the child is (paradoxically) "by nature" monstrous. That possibility is not at all merely academic, since severely "deformed" children may be isolated after birth or even killed; Locke quotes and comments on a case described by Giles Menage:

"When the abbot of Saint Martin," says he, "was born, he had so little the figure of a man, that it bespake him rather a monster. It was for some time under deliberation, whether he

[38]*Ibid.*, p. 128.
[39]*Ibid.*, p. 164.

should be baptized or no. However, he was baptized, and declared a man provisionally [till time should show what he would prove]. Nature had moulded him so untowardly, that he was called all his life the Abbot Malotru; i.e. ill-shaped. . . ." This child, we see, was very near being excluded out of the species of man, barely by his shape. He escaped very narrowly as he was; and it is certain, a figure a little more oddly turned had cast him, and he had been executed, as a thing not to be allowed to pass for a man.[40]

This passage from the *Essay*, though Sterne was doubtless familiar with it, has escaped, so far as I know, the notice of Sterne scholars. Yet the deliberation on baptism (and the resolution in favor of "provisional" baptism) strikingly resembles what occurs in Tristram's Dutch source (1.20), while the entire question is urgently germane to the Shandean condition. Note: "a thing not to be allowed to pass for a man." Somewhere a decision had to be made (how? by whom?) to dominate a process of figuration ("a figure a little more oddly turned") that would otherwise threaten to erase boundaries. Locke argues against the believers in archetypal essences who presume to know that the notion of "humanity" is determined not by arbitrary social convention but by "precise boundaries set by nature."[41] Yet Locke's argument, especially with its ambiguities about "nature," can hardly be counted upon to protect mutants from the sorts of situation he had so vividly just described.

Tristram, as if involved, quietly develops the problem: a disfiguring might occur at any stage in nature's processes, possibly in the production of a homunculus (as complete and well formed, Tristram protests—perhaps too much—"as my Lord Chancellor of England"; 1.2), possibly in its journey, in its gestation or, finally, as we have seen, in its delivery. Having stressed the rampant dangers all along not only of

[40]*Essay*, 3.6.26.
[41]*Ibid.*, 3.6.27.

maiming but of accidental death, Tristram cites a learned
Dutch source (in French and Latin) on the possibility of
baptizing homunculi in the womb, conditionally—"*sous condition.*" The term "*sous condition*" is reiterated when he "begs
to know" if the homunculi might be baptized when still in
the father, that is, before being escorted by the unreliable
animal spirits on the perilous journey toward the mother's
womb.[42] Should the little gentlemen "do well and come safe
into the world," Tristram goes on, they could again be baptized "*sous condition.*" In such a case, however, what could be
the *condition*? Might there be some doubt about whether or
not what finally comes out from the womb, if disfigured,
could be genuinely "human"? Note that (in the epigraph)
Locke imagines some hypothetical reader to be producing,
step by step, a monster and that in Tristram's case the problem of deformation is compounded and perhaps disguised
in that the act of bringing Tristram into the world seems to
have damaged him—if not by brain injuries, as the father
and uncle fear, then by having had his face crushed by the
forceps of Dr. Slop (3.16, 3.19, 3.27), whose real-life coun-
terpart wrote a notice, as earlier remarked, of a monstrous
child. That child, to cite the notice,

> had no Parts of Generation proper either to Male or Female,
> there not being the least appearance of such Organs at the
> Place where we should expect to find those Parts; the Child in
> every other Part was made as is common, except about half
> Way betwixt the Navel and the *Os pubis*, where [there] was a
> circular Orifice about an Inch Diameter, in which was a spongi-
> ous Substance resembling the End of the *Glans Penis* excori-
> ated; it did not project in the least from the Body, neither was
> it covered, but was quite bare and very sore and tender.[43]

[42]For the assumptions here, see Louis A. Landa, "The Shandean Homunculus: The Background of Sterne's 'Little Gentleman,'" in *Restoration
and Eighteenth-Century Literature*, ed. Carroll Camden (Chicago: University of
Chicago Press, 1963), pp. 49–68.

[43]John Burton, M.D., "An Account of a Monstrous Child," in *Medical Essays and Observations*, vol. 5, pt. 1 (Edinburgh: Ruddimans, 1742), pp.
338–39.

That the child's monstrosity should have to do with strange, absent, or misplaced genitals is of course curiously Shandean, and this text, along with the others mentioned, might be ventured as subtexts of *Tristram Shandy*.

II

Our reading of the Shandean text departs considerably from standard readings in that it stresses what they at most only hint at, namely that an aberrantly made and delivered Tristram seems to plead, in part by his very capacity to plead, that he, like the homunculus, is a "Gentleman"—so says the title page—and "our fellow creature" (1.2) and that he belongs to (presumably, comes from) the Shandy family. Furthermore, his beginning argument (that a homunculus has all the bodily articulations and thus all the rights of an adult human; 1.2) is a variation on and against Locke's suggestion that bounds of the "human" can never be established, that even a perfectly formed "human" body is not a necessary sign of some human "within." Although Tristram is squashed in his nose and possibly elsewhere as well, he need not be inhuman, for he is (if bizarrely) "rational" and has opinions: "Shall the want of a nose, or a neck, make a monster," Locke asks, "and put such issue out of the rank of men; the want of reason and understanding, not?"[44] We need not "talk at random about *man*," Locke continues, not quite consistently, once we abandon our jargon and "truly look."[45]

There can be, however, no simple looking at man, for the opacity of body interferes with our observance (so Tristram comments on Momus; 1.23); nor can a somehow nonrhetorical language "speak of things as they are,"[46] especially not in *Tristram Shandy*, which from the very outset is marked by

[44]*Essay*, 4.4.16.
[45]*Ibid.*
[46]*Essay*, 3.10.34.

rhetoricity: from an "obliquity" in his making that is "unaccountable" yet is described in great detail, Tristram Shandy's "course" shows "tokens of excentricity" (1.3, 21). In just that respect he should be Shandean, and his father might have offered an explanation for Tristram's "character": "all the SHANDY FAMILY were of an original character throughout" (1.21). Aside from whether ex-centricities can bear family resemblances, Walter Shandy "had his reasons" (perhaps excentric) for avoiding such an explanation. Genealogical identity depends on assured sexuality, but in *Tristram Shandy* resemblances are suspiciously rhetorical; even from his famous *ab ovo* start, Tristram—like his father—is interrupted: "*Pray, my dear,* quoth my mother, *have you not forgot to wind up the clock?*——Good G——! cried my father, making an exclamation, but taking care to moderate his voice at the same time,——*Did ever woman, since the creation of the world, interrupt a man with such a silly question?* Pray, what was your father saying?——Nothing" (1.1). All three questions, each as it were provoking the next, mark gaps, ruptures, and a dispersion of his "I," Tristram says, into a "quite different figure" (1.1). In response to a fictional (mis-)reader's question, "Nothing" is a beginning authorial effort to stop proliferating error, but the effort (as succeeding sentences will show) is ineffectual, while "Nothing" entangles various verbal and sexual performances in their negations.

The questioning fictional reader may be understandably puzzled, since Tristram begins ex-centrically with a substitution and reversal, that is, with what he wishes and what failed to happen—that "either my father or my mother, or indeed both of them, . . . had minded what they were about when they begot me" (1.1). In his "Nothing" a diffusion of meanings seems (already) beyond control: the father was saying nothing but was merely performing his marital duties; Tristram says "nothing" in hopes of dismissing the fictional reader's silly question, thereby avoiding awkward explanations. These possibilities, however "true," are also erroneous or ineffectual: the father does not say nothing (he speaks to Mrs. Shandy to stress, as Tristram does, the importance of the act), while Tristram's evasiveness only heightens a reader's persistence. In the entanglement of literally disrupted dissemination with disrupted speech, the "Nothing" leaves, so to speak, a mark: the father or mother ("indeed, both of them") conceived nothing, and the text gives signs that Tristram may exist only in some small unconvincing manner as a "name," hypothesis, or "mortal of . . . little consequence" (1.8).

Tristram would nonetheless like to claim, in and against disappointed logocentric hopes, some sort of self. Everywhere the mystique of authorship is thus both asserted and questioned: Tristram follows no man's rules and tells his story in his own digressive way (4.10, 8.1, 9.25), all the while having to make such an effort seem significant ("this is not so inconsiderable a thing"; 1.1). His hobby-horses and tiny homunculi must, like his "I," be rhetorically "explained" and amplified—an endeavor that, though playfully displayed as such, is for the same reason riskily self-subverting.

In one of Tristram's stories of Yorick, for instance, a group of scholars would explain the expostulation of Phutatorius (and Yorick's apparent trick) as having a "mystical meaning," while Tristram "as an historian" finds such speculation on the "cause and first spring" to be "as groundless as the dreams of philosophy" (4.27). He recounts his version of the "causes" quite simply: a hot chestnut, having fallen into Phutatorius's pants, is picked up by Yorick. Yet if as one contemporary reader, David Hume, would argue, cause-effect relations are habitual associations rather than necessary connections, Tristram is less than convincing in tracing an effect back to its antecedents, which always in turn require explaining; despite Tristram's ironic counterclaims (9.20), events can never quite be known.

Tristram proposes, even so, "to do exact justice to every creature brought upon the stage of this dramatic work" (1.10). "Justice" is traditionally crucial to epistemology and politics: what is "just" is correct, true, and humane, not only reporting disorder but reordering it in accord with what "should" be. Conventional rhetoric enters here: the necessary condition for metaphor (the class of all figures, according to Aristotle) is an awareness of resemblance or likeness, which is also the necessary condition for "proper" mimesis. Metaphor, however, discovers resemblances by ignoring differences—its "truth" is erroneous or, in Derrida's formulation, metaphor "is possible sense as a possibility of non-truth, . . . the moment of detour in which truth can still be lost"; contrary to the dream of metaphysics, there can be no non-metaphoric or "outside" ground from which metaphor can be valorized.[47]

The Shandean text in its rhetoricity plays upon that situation, heightened with "hobby-horses" as the delusively constant grounds for metaphoric extensions of self. Since Tristram's hobby-horse is his writing, he (or we) might be tempted to privilege it, for it apparently does justice to other hobby-horses—it "places" them by acts of parodying, representing, explaining, and defending. Tristram stresses, indeed, his claim for doing "justice": though his father's argument for a man midwife fails utterly to persuade Mrs. Shandy, Tristram will "endeavour to do it justice" (2.19; cf. 8.34); Tristram's relations with Jenny may seem irregular, but "All I plead for is strict justice" (1.18); the story of Uncle Toby's amours in book 9 is an attempt to justify that gentleman's behavior.[48] The doing of authorial justice, however, seems no more extensive or effectively rhetorical than other

[47]"White Mythology," trans. F. T. C. Moore, *NLH* 4 (1974):42.
[48]On Tristram's "testimony" as juridical, see William B. Piper, *Laurence Sterne* (New York: Twayne, 1965), pp. 21–30.

hobby-horses, which in their ludicrousness, indeed, reflect back upon Tristram's efforts.

Consider Tristram's explanation of the "hobby-horse" idea in reference to Yorick's hobby-horse as a "real" (Cervantine) horse. Tristram offers to rectify, with his story, false stories propagated by a gossipy village against Yorick. As a forensic *auctor*, Tristram strives for corrective truth ("the truth of the story was as follows", "in plain truth", "to speak the truth"; 1.10–12). But there can be no normative "truth" (or "real" hobby-horse) for hobby-horses; oddly perhaps, Yorick's most troublesome feature had been that he, Yorick, told the truth, without rhetorical falsifications: "*Yorick* had no impression but one, and that was what arose from the nature of the deed spoken of; which impression he would usually translate into plain *English* without any periphrasis———, . . . if it was a dirty action,———without more ado,———The man was a dirty fellow" (1.11).

Although Tristram would defend Yorick by proving him to be in some sense innocent, Yorick as jester can hardly be innocent of tropes: his comments terminate "in a *bon mot*" and he is sandalous, indeed, in his peculiar version of "plain *English*,"[49] for as Tristram remarks: "fatality attends the actions of some men: Order them as they will, they pass thro' a certain medium which . . . twists and refracts them from their true directions" (1.10). That "certain medium" pervades *Tristram Shandy*—"fatality" includes more than "some men" and is virtually the only "truth" that Tristram's story can exemplify. If Yorick is warned by Eugenius of an economics of jest (the jestee will demand compensation), the warning, supposedly so "realistic" and "confirmed" (by warfare and Yorick's death), is also allegorically hyperbolic (in "REVENGE," "MALICE," etc.) and in mourning ("Alas, poor YORICK!"; 1.12),

---

[49]"Plain English" is a favorite Lockean term; see for instance the *First Treatise of Government*, in Laslett, 3.18, 6.69, 9.111 (hereafter, *First Treatise*).

which is not only a citation but a narrative analepsis (Yorick shortly reappears).

The agent of these rhetorical tricks, instead of being dispersed among surrogate authors, as in *Don Quixote* (alluded to at every turn), is described as a writing figure who is quixotic in his singularity: the effort to write is a quaint combat, in and despite its ironized nostalgia, against other hobbyhorses (as noncommunicative) and against a doubtfully phallocentric father.

III

The father, Walter Shandy, with his "philosophical" schemes, hinders rather than helps Tristram: he seems to pass on, so to speak, his productive inability in unclear trains of misfortune and heavy artillery (4.19). Tristram tries nonetheless to equalize himself with his apparent human antecedents by suggesting that his crippling misfortunes resemble and are linked to theirs. Rhetorically muted by affection, his opposing self is inscribed in figures of contrast and analogy that can never quite be secure, and so his mimetic ventures must be more telling than their possible effects.

The scene of the son-father opposition, for instance, can never quite be located, even though Tristram has his "opinion" of his father as "philosopher" (he "would see nothing in the light in which others placed it") and he describes, in careful antithesis, his father's eloquence (it was his "strength———for he was by nature eloquent,———and his weakness———for he was hourly a dupe to it"; 2.19, 5.3). We may wonder whether Tristram is less of a dupe to his own rhetoric, especially in his boasts of writing by no known rules; the plights indeed of father and son may be intertwined in a strange lack of difference.

Tristram indicates, to be sure, that he has displaced his father: Walter deferred the repair of an annoyingly squeaky door hinge, which "shall be mended this reign" (3.21). "This" presumably is the temporality of Tristram's writing: "From this moment I am to be considered as heir-apparent to the *Shandy* family——and it is from this point properly that the story of my LIFE and my OPINIONS sets out"; "From the first moment I sat down to write . . .has a cloud been insensibly gathering over my father" (4.32, 3.28). The "this" and "moment," however, are for the same reason suspect, and we have little more to go on than that Walter advances a particular brand of justice: nothing less than "the welfare of nations" is meant to persuade Mrs. Shandy not to go to London to give birth to her child ("the current of men and money towards the metropolis, upon one frivolous errand or another,——set in so strong,——as to become dangerous to our civil rights; 1.18; cf. 3.42). But if Walter's hypotheses find their supposed corroboration in public affairs, they turn out disastrously in the "lesser" affairs of family life ("Never did the parlour-door open——but his philosophy or his principles fell a victim to it"; 3.21).

The ideological stake is hinted at in reworkings of Locke's critique of Filmer's *De Patriarcha*[50] in the *First Treatise of Government*. Tristram informs us that with regard to retaining the balance of power, Walter "was entirely of Sir *Robert Filmer's* opinion" (1.18). This surely warrants attention, since Filmer (in Locke's paraphrase) argues that on the basis of a God-given right, a father—from Adam onward—could "take or alienate [his children's] Estates, sell, castrate or use their Persons as he pleases."[51] Locke strongly questions whether the Bible justifies assumptions of the absolute power of fathers over children as kings over subjects. When Filmer would bestow the title of Father (in "Habit," not in

---

[50]This text's influence has been generally overlooked; see, however, Wilfred Watson, "The Fifth Commandment: Some Allusions to Sir Robert Filmer's Writings in *Tristram Shandy*," *MLN*, 62 (1947):234–40.

[51]Locke, *First Treatise*, 2.9.

"Act") upon Adam without Adam's having to beget, the practical Locke objects that "in plain English, He had actually no Title at all."[52] When Filmer allows, on the other hand, that absolute fatherly power comes from begetting,[53] Locke wonders (in a passage we can imagine to strike both Walter and Tristram) how much knowledge the transmission of life can be considered to provide:

> To give Life to that which has yet no being is to frame and make a living Creature. . . . If any one thinks himself an Artist at this, let him number up the parts of his Childs Body . . . , tell me their Uses and Operations, and when the living and rational Soul began to inhabit this curious Structure, when Sense began, and how this Engine which he has framed Thinks and Reasons: If he made it, let him, when it is out of order, mend it, at least tell wherein the defects lie.[54]

The father can hardly be given full responsibility for (or authority over) his children if they are made, as often happens, "without the intention, and often against the Consent and will of the Begetter."[55] Such a possibility indeed, must have been in Walter's mind when he drew up the marriage contract with Mrs. Shandy (1.15).

However much, at any rate, Filmer (and Walter Shandy; 5.31) would like to qualify the female's role in child production, Locke (who would stress "labor," after all, as the basis for property) does not. Filmer, Locke notices, evades a crucial problem by quoting the Bible incompletely; thus every time Filmer urges "honour thy father," Locke adds "and mother."[56] For if obedience to the mother is also at issue, the father's privileged position is shaken, and the child's allegiances may become divided or indecisive (in *Tristram*

[52]*Ibid.*, 3.18.
[53]*Ibid.*, 6.50.
[54]*Ibid.*, 6.53.
[55]*Ibid.*, 6.54.
[56]*Ibid.*, 2.6, 6.55, 6.60–6.63.

Shandy, we recall, the mother from the outset contends with the father and later may even—despite the theologians—be "of kin to her child"; 4.29–30). Filmer is so insistent to link paternal with royal power, Locke says, that under Filmer's patriarchal government "there will be as many Sovereigns as there are Fathers"; actual fathers, however, cannot be given much regal credit for what they have done: the act is momentary, and, as Tristram will wistfully wonder in his very first sentence, though adding a mother to this question of Locke's, "What Father of a Thousand, when he begets a Child, thinks farther?"[57]

The problem does not end with begetting. Although Filmer would like each proper heir to become "as much Lord as his Father was," he is unable to designate a rule by which heirs are to be chosen, and so Locke can pose (once again) a succession of unanswerable questions: "I go on then to ask whether in the inheriting of this Paternal Power, . . . the Grand-Son by a Daughter, hath a Right before a Nephew by a Brother? Whether the Grand-Son by the Eldest Son, being an Infant, before the Younger Son a Man and able? Whether the Daughter before the Uncle? . . . Whether an Elder Son by a Concubine, before a Younger Son by a Wife?"[58] Such possible undecidability of status, in the very relations that words (Locke says) can so clearly designate,[59] is not without bearing on Tristram, who becomes his father's heir in an act of words—"from this moment I am to be considered as heir-apparent to the Shandy family——and it is from this point properly that the story of my LIFE and my OPINIONS sets out" (4.32). Can "this point properly" somehow cancel Tristram's earlier (improper?) "beginning" and Walter's involvement with it?

---

[57]*Ibid.*, 6.65, 6.54.
[58]*Ibid.*, 9.119, 123.
[59]*Essay*, 2.28.2. These Locke calls "natural relations," adding that they are not fitted "to the truth and extent of things."

What we have called the son-father "opposition" is complicated in that Walter's hobby-horse, despite its peculiarities, is
only arguably different from others, including Tristram's.
Recall the activity of inscribed readers in Tristram's discourse. Recall, too, the reactions to Tristram's boyhood accident: when a window sash falls upon his urinating genitals,
the nurse holding him is terrified: "————Nothing is left,
cried *Susannah*,————nothing is left————for me, but to
run my country.————" (5.17). Tristram seems willing, by
the "Nothing," so like his earlier one, to make suggestions
about what occurred, for although he, if anyone, should be
able to clarify the issue, he for the same reason perhaps least
of all could do so. There is at any rate much discussion
(among the Shandys) as to whether what is left could be
called circumcision or (among the villagers) something more
(or less). Uncle Toby, to be sure, proposes amicably to put a
stop to unfavorable gossip:

> ————I would shew him publickly, said my uncle *Toby*, at the
> market cross.
> ————'Twill have no effect, said my father. [6.14].

What a shortened—or missing—phallus can be called
would not be resolved by an *argumentum ad rem*, since the
(non-)*rem* would only incite further—and interminable—
debate. If moreover Dr. Burton's note on a monstrous child
is relevant, one story may disguise another, and Tristram's
accident may indefinitely already have occurred. In this,
however, Tristram's hobbled or hobby-horsical condition resembles others, and the quasi-castration undecidably marks
a rivalry-identification (if that) not only with the father, as
we might expect, but with all the Shandys. Hypotheses and
war plans are poor machinelike proceedings against
"chance" happenings. And although Tristram somewhat
archly denies that he needs "mechanical help" (1.24), he,
too, is possessed of a machine—his pen.

Changeling Fathering: *Tristram Shandy*

With its wishful eroticism, Tristram's writing is an act of flawed sexuality: in haste and trouble his instrument strokes the paper, emits fluids, and leaves what marks it may. His pen—his shortened "penis"—is recklessly moved about, scattering its ink. It governs Tristram and not he it, he says; he will throw it into the fire or relinquish it; it is part of his book, his health, his moods; it is the sluggish channel for his thoughts; it gives him military and sexual power over the reader; it journeys as he does, and becomes fatigued (3.28, 9.13, 6.6, 4.32, 9.24, 7.1, 6.17, 7.43). Unclear in all this is giving or losing as producing or appropriating; the "effect" or nonmark of Tristram's wound can never be settled, and as dissimulator or trace it eludes the binaries castration/ anticastration (circumcision) or truth/falsehood. If we recall Nietzsche's affection for *Tristram Shandy*, we might also recall Derrida's Nietzschean reading of "woman" as nonidentity, nonfigure, dissimulation, "truth" (in quotes):

> "Woman"—the word made epoch—no more believes in castration's exact opposite [*à l'envers franc*], anti-castration, than in castration. . . . She knows that such a reversal would only take away all possibility of simulation [*simulacre*], that it would return in truth to the same and install her more surely than ever in . . . phallogocentrism. . . . "Woman" has need of castration's effect, without which she could not seduce or incite desire— but obviously she does not believe in it.[60]

There is no simple inversion of "phallogocentrism" in the Shandean text, but instead a dizzying rhetoricity that leaves no authoring "self" intact; a quasi-"castrated" ("authoring") Tristram as "woman"—in quotes—is inhuman and human, monster and foetus-"Gentleman," or perhaps a changeling, a substitute left by stealth in (as) changing. In the epigraph Locke hypothesizes a "well-shaped changeling" only to have

---

[60] *Spurs/Eperons*, trans. Barbara Harlow (Chicago: University of Chicago Press, 1973), p. 60; translation modified.

it change, that is, to have it more "truly" a changeling—or a monster. Can, then, a changeling "belong" in the family—or story line? What is the "cause" for him as "effect"? And is not the very notion of "belonging" being inevitably laid bare?

With Tristram as the last, impotent, and dying member of the Shandy line, that question is poignant—and displaced. We may thus be tempted to ignore it and to respond to the story as persuasion or sentiment rather than as figurality. If so, the narrative "rhetoric"—the digressions, interruptions, rearrangements—will all give "proof" of a space of author-ial "freedom" and of an "independent" reality of persons or events that any authorial efforts (asterisks, diagrams, black or blank pages) can only approximate. Although the very lack of adequate signs may thus be turned into a "proof" of external reality, that "reality" is so crossed by chance (so "real") as to stage the need for deviously indecent (jocosely "interesting," trickily "profound") stories. Recuperation and deconstruction play upon each other, generating a continual tease about possible kinship between the teller and his fam-ily(-tale), the tale and its scene, the rhetorician and our responses.

Notice for instance how the tie between "agency" or con-tent and emotional response is accidental or unpredictable:

Are we not here now, continued the corporal, (striking the end of his stick perpendicularly upon the floor, so as to give an idea of health and stability)————and are we not————(dropping his hat upon the ground) gone! in a moment!————'Twas infinitely striking! *Susannah* burst into a flood of tears.————We are not stocks and stones.————*Jonathan, Obadiah*, the cook-maid, all melted. . . .

I said, "we were not stocks and stones"————'tis very well. I should have added, nor are we angels, I wish we were,————but men cloathed with bodies, and governed by our imaginations. [5.7]

Since our "author" interjects comments on the scene to his fictional readers, the "I" that takes up Trim's discourse is indeterminate. Trim, Tristram: each names the other as figure or simulacrum, as mere contraction or mere amplification. It would be all too easy, by so tracing anagrams, to speculate on schemes of opposition and complicity—the sentimentals Trim-Toby-Tristram "against" the less humane Walter—Widow Wadman, and (somewhat to the side) the relatively neutral Yorick or Mrs. Shandy. For although "selves" in *Tristram Shandy* are interfigural, such configurations are implausible to the extent that Shandean valorizations and "communications" are vertiginously ironized.[61] Any notion of "communication" is doubtful, since in trains of thoughts all agreements may be hobby-horsical (mis-)understandings (4.12, 6.2).

Tristram exploits, indeed, the doubtfulness of communication to set up illusions of authorial presence: he converses with foregrounded readers—"Madam" and "Sir"—for whose sake he interrupts and explains his story. The fictional readers, however, seem theatrical (nameless, they are described exclusively in their responses to Tristram), and a staged authorial appearance undercuts at least as much as it nourishes illusions of "communication." The gesture that makes Tristram "available" to his fictional readers is likely to distance "us" as readers, if only because he in effect blocks "our" responses by means of theirs even while implying that our reactions, like theirs, could be drawn rhetorically into (as) his figures.

Even Tristram, however, is blocked (not without consequences for "us") from the family that he supposedly so intimately knows and represents. He claims offhandedly to have had conversations with Uncle Toby (1.3), but these are never directly quoted, and Tristram has no immediate relation

---

[61]On vertigo, see Lanham, *"Tristram Shandy"*, pp. 46–47.

with his family members: he never holds a single spoken exchange with any of them but only watches, so to speak, in silence or cries out to them in unheard anguish (6.28). This poignantly reiterates the gaps of pastness, illegitimacy, and death at the very moments Tristram most apparently overcomes them. It gives no sign of self or Shandean relations except as figurations that are necessarily nonappropriative. Could it be that Tristram's "life" is nothing but his "opinions" that he lived? Does the changeling-foetus, his nine chapters miming the nine months of a human gestation, plead quite persuasively that he belongs? His overdetermined and digressive story suspiciously telescopes all "life" between an allegorized flight from "Death" and a long-deferred "birth" the evidence for which, despite extensive details, remains circumstantial.

This circumstantiality is indirectly at issue in the nominally culminating *amours* in which Uncle Toby dictates a list of Mrs. Wadman's virtues to Trim, who writes "HUMANITY - - - - - thus" (9.31). Evidence for the widow's humanity (her continual inquiries about Uncle Toby's phallic wound) turns out to be evidence against it, and Tristram, in recording this, presumably does "justice." He cannot claim, even so, to enter himself, by his ability to recognize a supposed absence of humanity, into the ranks of being human or a "Gentleman." Tristram's title page may thus have some untold basis for its inscription of "Gentleman," or else his rhetoric is deceptively forensic. For the widow is no less "human" in her scheming concupiscence than Uncle Toby in his modesty: had not the Shandean text all along played upon just such pluralities? With its doubtful horses, cocks, and bulls, it is neither "SYSTEM" nor "BREVIARY" nor "FACT" (8.8). And it moves so far in loosening the "humanity" concept from hierarchical oppositions that the concept becomes, perhaps, changelinglike.

6

Half-Breeding:
Absalom, Absalom!

They (the niggers) were not it, not what you wanted to
hit; . . . you knew that when you hit them you would just
be hitting a child's toy balloon with a face painted on it. . . .
—*Absalom, Absalom!*

Two not quite compatible features mark William
Faulkner's *Absalom, Absalom!* On the one hand, the entire
story seems governed, so the tellers claim, by an economics:
Mr. Coldfield's conscience operates according to a "demand
balance of spiritual solvency" (50);[1] renegadery or outrage
must be compensated "to clear the books, pay the check"
(68; cf. 18); Sutpen, believing that he has recompensed his
first wife, is surprised to see Bon's face, since he has "paid
[it] off" (265); Clytie believes about Henry that "whatever he
done, me and Judith and him have paid it out" (370); fate is
a "*Creditor*" with a "*hand . . . on his* [Sutpen's *shoulder*" (182),
and some things "have to be . . . , just to balance the books"
(325). On the other hand, however, the text is punctuated
repeatedly by phrases of not-knowing: "they did not know"

---

[1]References are by page number to *Absalom, Absalom!* (New York: Random House, 1936). Any italics in the citations are Faulkner's. I have indicated with double quotation marks passages which should properly be indicated with single quotation marks within double quotation marks, since they are narrated by one of the characters. I do this simply for convenience, and not to minimize the intriguing phenomenon of multiple citationality in Faulkner's text.

(34); "they were never to know" (43); "It just does not explain" (100); "And who knows?" (120); "she didn't know . . . because he didn't know" (132); *"knowing nothing, able to learn nothing"* (135); "Nobody ever did know for certain" (259); "a fact . . . foisted upon me without my knowledge" (273).

Do some sorts of not-knowing, we might ask, escape all economics, or can some sorts of economics include not-knowing? Might not-knowing require a speculation on investments for which the return is inestimable and even unidentifiable? And might not these questions themselves be questionable? At every turn, after all, any balancing—indeed, any system by which balancing might be possible—is strangely subverted by an unassimilable remainder ("You've got one nigger . . . Sutpen left"; 378) which "is" both in and apart from the system (Sutpen's "eugenic" breeding) which would exclude or even account for it. The stakes are considerable, for telling is an accounting for—a re-counting of—events that in this case involve an aspect of the logocentric strategy called "economimesis" whereby the animal or inhuman is subordinated to the human,[2] and whereby, in the Faulknerian text, so the characters often believe, the Negro race can and should be subordinated to the white race.

As "economics," however, mimesis in *Absalom, Absalom!* is

[2]Jacques Derrida, "Economimesis," trans. R. Klein, *Diacritics* 11, no. 2 (1981):5. In this hierarchy, the "genius," according to Kant and Romantic expression theory, escapes from the confines of slavish imitation, mercenary art, and the economy of exchange. But the poet or genius, precisely in his unlimited, overflowing abundance of producing, becomes the delegate and faithful image of the producing God. There is thus a mimetic identification at the basis of "antimimetic" theories, and "the relation of alterity between a restricted economy and a general economy is above all not . . . of opposition" (*ibid.*, 12). This has bearing on Faulkner's text: Sutpen might be associated with Romantic "genius" or heroism in his apparently godlike freedom from ordinary ways (in building his house, the French architect has to restrain Sutpen's ambitions; 38). But later, and still in the interest of an eventual abundance, Sutpen as moral reckoner and shopkeeper haggles over mistakes and small coins (269, 281). Economimesis turns out to be questionable on all levels.

indeterminately excessive and incomplete, and this indeterminacy jeopardizes claims for the story's pertinence as history or politics. It puts into question not only the efforts of narrators who may wish to tell why the South lost the Civil War or what the South is like (11, 174), but those of commentators who would rather read *Absalom, Absalom!* as some sort of statement about Southern history than as an allegory, perhaps, of why the South cannot have a history of itself. For what the story continually dramatizes, despite the tellers' contrary desires, is a gap between signs and referents that is either unbroached or else broached in efforts that are patently factitious.

I

Let us recall, as a tentative concession to those who might oppose this view, a Faulknerian statement, hardly elusive, that might seem relevantly political and Southern: "If it came to fighting I'd fight for Mississippi against the United States even if it meant going out into the street and shooting Negroes."[3] Faulkner doubted, amid a subsequent public furor, that he had made any such statement, insisting that many remarks attributed to him were ones "no sober man would make and . . . no sane man believe."[4] Indeed he was apparently offering a "worst possible" scenario; he was indulging in hyperbole. At what point, though, can such hyperbole be creditably defigured into some proper statement on race relations? Is a necessary part perhaps of any truly Faulknerian statement its figurality?

Commentators have often found themselves helpless, after all, to extract a "consistent" Faulknerian viewpoint on race.

[3]Interview with Russell W. Howe, *The Reporter* 14 (March 22, 1956):19.
[4]Letter to *Time* 67 (April 23, 1956):12; cited in William Faulkner, *Essays. Speeches and Public Letters*, ed. James B. Meriwether (New York: Random House, 1965), p. 226.

Thus Charles D. Peavy, who sets for himself the task of making an "appraisal of Faulkner's views on the Negro," carefully shies away from the novels and stories, and even then notices that "almost every sentence contradicts the one preceding it"; more generally, he never explores why Faulkner "has been seen as a radical reactionary and a sentimental traditionalist; he has been blamed for making the Negro a scapegoat for the destruction of the legendary South; and he has been called a bigot and a 'nigger lover.'"[5]

Binary oppositions such as these, if essential to an assessment of Faulkner's "position," seem to mock their proponents and to generate unending polemics. The issue of miscegenation proves particularly perplexing. In *Absalom, Absalom!*, Irving Howe states, "there is a whole range of responses to miscegenation, . . . and it is quite impossible to say with any assurance where Faulkner's final sympathy, or the final stress of the novel itself, lies."[6] John Irwin, again, begins his reading of Faulkner with a citation about miscegenation but translates Bon's blackness into Quentin's shadow self and never otherwise deals with miscegenation, while Melvin Seiden tells us that although "Faulkner has created his world around a core of traditional and unargued racism, . . . everything that is fine in the book compels us to offer resistance."[7] Whether the "racism" is traditional or Southern is surely arguable;[8] in any case, Seiden goes on, "racism is a smokescreen, a red herring. . . . It is not miscegenation, . . . not the thing itself but its chimerical, hallucinatory force that Faulkner is dealing with."[9] Seiden points to a concluding

[5]Charles D. Peavy, *Go Slow Now: Faulkner and the Race Question* (Eugene: University of Oregon Press, 1971), pp. 13, 46.

[6]*William Faulkner* (New York: Vintage, 1951), p. 128.

[7]John Irwin, *Doubling and Incest/Repetition and Revenge* (Baltimore: Johns Hopkins University Press, 1975), p. 28; Melvin Seiden, "Faulkner's Ambiguous Negro," *Massachusetts Review* 4 (1962–63):678.

[8]See Cleanth Brooks, *William Faulkner: The Yoknapatawpha Country* (New Haven: Yale University Press, 1963), pp. 297–99.

[9]Seiden, "Faulkner's Ambiguous Negro," 678.

passage in *Absalom, Absalom!* in which Shreve comments on what is left of Sutpen's dynasty—the miscegenated idiot Jim Bond: "I think that in time the Jim Bonds are going to conquer the western hemisphere. Of course it won't quite be in our time and of course as they spread toward the poles they will bleach out again like the rabbits and birds do. . . . [But] in a few thousand years, I who regard you will also have sprung from the loins of African kings" (378). Seiden, in reaction, succumbs to what he had just described as hallucinatory:

> the logic of the Sutpen tale does seem to confirm the fearful vision of mongrelization. . . . Is Faulkner playing with us here? This idea is so irritating that it would be less painful to know with reasonable certainty that Shreve at this point *is* Faulkner, and be done with it. But Faulkner does not resolve the problem, nor can I. . . . Shreve means [the words he says,] . . . and Faulkner does not provide us with any ground for necessarily discounting or discrediting them.[10]

Notice "discounting" and "discrediting": the commentator would like to balance out what he finds unknowable, "fearful," "painful," and "irritating." Yet it is just this sort of operation, we remarked, that the text repeatedly puts into question.

Faulkner can say, to be sure, that regarding the problem of Negro status, "there is too much talk of right," and a commentator like James Guetti can argue that Sutpen's exclusion of Bon is not a social issue.[11] Yet despite such indications that conventional moral and political categories may be less than relevant, Faulkner (certainly the public Faulkner)

---

[10]*Ibid.*, 684.

[11]*Faulkner at West Point*, ed. J. Fant III and R. Ashley (New York: Random House, 1964), p. 88; James Guetti, *The Limits of Metaphor* (Ithaca: Cornell University Press, 1967), p. 88: "Sutpen could have either accepted Bon and concealed his Negro blood or refused to accept him and proclaimed it. In either case a merely social design would have been unimpaired."

speaks directly to logocentric sentiments when he gloriously proclaims in his Nobel Prize speech that even in some "last ding-dong of doom, [man will be more than a] puny inexhaustible voice": man "is immortal, not because he alone among creatures has an inexhaustible voice, but because he has a soul, a spirit capable of compassion and sacrifice and endurance."[12] Although voice and soul are thus connected in timeless self-presence, when such rhetoric is voiced by Faulknerian characters, its value is often strongly doubted. In such instances the text may be logocentric *and yet* deconstructed—two aspects that cannot be related as simple oppositions in or against what is calculably economic or traditionally knowable.[13]

Let us elaborate. Economics is a managment of the *oikos*, of the house as one's own or as one's line in the regal sense. Sutpen, however, is undone precisely in his efforts to control a genealogical line that as his "own" is never straight or clear but instead deviant, or troped. Sutpen's dream is of undisturbed self-presence in which he would be "even after he would become dead, still there, still watching the fine grandsons springing as far as the eye could reach" (271), and the criterion by which grandsons are "fine" is that none in the house, physical or dynastic, be of mixed blood. Notice, however, that the house is erected on a "black foundation" (78) and that miscegenation molests self-presence partly because poor whites are at least as painfully ambiguous in social status as half-breeds and even less defined hierarchically than blacks ("Who him [Jones], calling us niggers?"; 281). Sutpen was rejected from the rich white plantation owner's door as

---

[12]"Address upon Receiving the Nobel Prize for Literature," repr. in *Essays, Speeches and Public Letters*, p. 120.

[13]Joseph Blotner writes in *Faulkner: A Biography*, vol. 2 (New York: Random House, 1974), that the Nobel Prize address "was a stirring rhetorical statement, but how had William Faulkner arrived at this position of seeming faith and affirmation after the great novels had appeared to say the very opposite?" (p. 1366). "Seeming," "appeared": "the very opposite" is somehow inadequate.

if he, Sutpen, were a presumptuous black: both black slaves and white squatters were laborers or "brutish" (235–36), and any difference between them can only be deceptively established by separating and privileging, as Sutpen does in his design, the self-made white boss over the indiscernible half-breed.

Any such efforts are marked by rhetoricity: despite having been planned methodically, they become dissemination. Sutpen would speak by doing in the sense of Giambattista Vico's early Roman nobles, who established dynasties to stand out against a "confusion of human seeds," against a primeval state "not distinguished by marriages."[14] Sanctioned Roman nuptial rites vested an inheritable family name or *nomos* to be transmitted by the father; any family member thereafter would be a patrician—"one '*qui potest nomine ciere patrem*,' 'who can name his father.'"[15] Roman nobles would never contract marriages with plebs, since any offspring would become "*secum ipsa discors*, which is as much to say a monster of mixed and twofold nature."[16] Thomas Sutpen, just so, would preclude on the male side what he considers to be a "mixed monster." If offspring bear a metonymic and metaphoric relation to their parents (contiguity, with birth, becomes resemblance),[17] Sutpen wants only controlled or proper figures as his line—his progeny, name, story—and to that end tries vainly and unceasingly to substitute wives for wives, children for children. Sutpen nonetheless in his design (and the tellers, too, we shall notice, in theirs) half breeds, that is, breeds incompletely, "impurely," or by some somatic erring produces half-breeds, a process both as and against self-deconstruction in which "he" is turned endlessly

---

[14]*The New Science*, trans. T. G. Bergin and M. H. Fisch (Ithaca: Cornell University Press, 1968), paragraph 17.

[15]*Ibid.*, paragraphs 110, 530.

[16]*Ibid.*, paragraph 567.

[17]Jean Laplanche, *Life and Death in Psychoanalysis*, trans. J. Mehlman (Baltimore: Johns Hopkins University Press, 1967), p. 139.

away, as from the door of the white master he would rival mimetically.

As in (or between) other selves, the conflict is a matter not of difference but of *différance*, and thus one cannot argue, except unconvincingly, as for example John Irwin does, that any figure, including Quentin, "is the central narrator . . . , because the other three only function as narrators in relation to Quentin."[18] For Quentin's mind especially has been so inscribed by other tellings that it may no longer be his; he cannot free himself from hearing the story and has no distinguishable authorial voice even with apparently different knowledge: new information all too easily becomes part of the same old discourse in which tellers (as they sometimes notice) sound just like one another (12, 211, 261–62, 277). In this context, a theory of psychological doubling (that Quentin's life story, say, provides a model for the Henry-Bon relationship[19]) is necessarily limited, since it assumes a splitting of self rather than an indeterminate fragmentation in which no self, even divided or doubled, can adequately be specified. Irwin contends, on the basis of an avowedly Freudian reading, that Quentin "identifies with" both Henry and Bon: "Bon represents Quentin's unconsciously motivated desire for his sister Candace, while Henry represents the conscious repression or punishment of that desire."[20] It is precisely such concepts as "identify" and "represent," however, that the Faulknerian and Freudian texts at various points call radically into question, and if this questioning is not to be ignored, doubling cannot simply be inscribed as econo-mimesis but only as some nonoppositional play of oppositions, as in the Derridean reading of the relations between the pleasure and reality principles: "it is the same *différant* . . . But the structure of the *différance* may then open the

[18]Irwin, *Doubling*, p. 26.
[19]*Ibid.*, p. 28.
[20]*Ibid.*

way to an alterity even more irreducible than that of opposition."[21]

II

Such an alterity, let us venture, characterizes *Absalom, Absalom!*, which we will thus read as marked by a nonoppositional double registration—by on the one hand a ratiocinative recounting of events, but on the other hand by circumstances hinted at tacitly, somatically, symptomatically. The first moves according to schemes such as Sutpen's design, Miss Rosa's "might-have-been" or Mr. Compson's hypotheses, the second moves according to forces of instinct, black blood, and inadmissible genealogies. Conflict between the two is generally concealed or deferred: Faulkner's characters, Jean-Jacques Mayoux observes, do not usually know what is done even at the moment the body does it, and hence consciousness "gets out of order, erratically moves ahead or lags behind the act . . . of the body."[22]

The plottings are comparable, let us suppose, not only to the reality and pleasure principles, but to the systems *conscious-preconscious* and *unconscious*, for which Freud offered a number of never quite sufficient analogies. The "unconscious" involves inferences about "manifestations which I notice in myself and do not know how to link up with the rest of my mental life [and which] must be judged as if they belonged to someone else."[23] Thus the possibility of a double "registration": when a mental act is transferred from the unconscious to the conscious-preconscious system, this transposition may involve "a fresh registration comparable to a sec-

[21]Derrida, *La carte postale* (Paris: Flammarion, 1980), p. 302.

[22]"The Creation of the Real in Faulkner," in *William Faulkner: Three Decades of Criticism*, ed. F. Hoffman and O. Vickery (New York: Harcourt Brace, 1963), p. 162.

[23]Sigmund Freud, "The Unconscious," in *General Psychological Theory*, ed. P. Rieff (New York: Collier, 1963), p. 120.

153

ond record [*Niederschrift*] . . . situated, moreover, in a fresh locality."[24] This formulation, as Derrida shows, is not discarded but is reworked as scriptive possibilities in which verbal phenomena are given a place that they are far from dominating; if dreams as *différance* are a lithography before the words or "logic" of consciousness, they are never simply retranscribable, and any transition to consciousness is in a writing that "in its very secondariness is originary and irreducible."[25]

Although Freudian concepts belong to the history of metaphysics,[26] binaries such as unconscious/conscious or somatic/psychic are indeterminate: repression—"something between flight and condemnation"—is known by substitute formations and symptoms which repression does not merely "coincide with" or "produce."[27] In such a situation, certain "derivatives of the unconscious" may "unite in themselves opposite features" and "by our . . . judgment [*für unser Urteil*]" possess all characteristics of consciousness:

> Thus they belong according to their qualities to the system Pcs, but in actual fact to the Uncs. Their origin [*Herkunft*] remains decisive for the fate [*Schicksal*] they will undergo. We may compare them [*Man muss sie . . . vergleichen*] with those human half-breeds [*Mischlingen menschlicher Rassen*] who, taken all round, resemble [*gleichen*] white men, but betray [*verraten*] their colored descent by some striking feature or other, on account of which they are excluded from society.[28]

We may be surprised here not only at the *vergleichen-gleichen* parallelism and the force of *man muss* but at the general ease

---

[24]*Ibid.*, p. 123; German from the *Gesammelte Werke* (London: Imago, 1946), vol. 10, p. 273.

[25]"Freud and the Scene of Writing," in *Writing and Difference*, trans. A. Bass (Chicago: University of Chicago Press, 1978), p. 212.

[26]*Ibid.*, p. 197.

[27]"Repression," in Rieff, *General Psychological Theory*, pp. 111–12.

[28]"The Unconscious," p. 138; *Gesammelte Werke*, vol. 10, pp. 289–90.

with which the narrator sketches the role of the white man anxious to retain social boundaries and sharply looking out for any telltale signs of racial origin that might determine the half-breed's *Schicksal*. *Mischlingen* do not properly "belong"—they are mongrels or hybrids, and here they imitate whiteness so insidiously that unless they "betray" themselves (or are betrayed) *für unser Urteil*, they threaten to invade the territory of consciousness and to erase valorized differences.

Precisely in the *Mischling* or half-breed, the Faulknerian text continues unabashedly the (at this point) somewhat reserved Freudian interrogation. Starting indeed with how the Faulknerian, like the Freudian, text questions "unconsciousness" as eventually full or present, let us notice how the half-breed as "trace" functions in that questioning.

III

Everywhere in *Absalom, Absalom!*, a "self"—or any "I" and its story—is doubted as unifier, as memory or perception. Quentin is "not a being, an entity, he [is] a commonwealth" (12), and for Miss Rosa,

> there is no such thing as memory: the brain recalls just what the mus-
> cles grope for: no more, no less: and its resultant sum is usually incor-
> rect and false and worthy only of the name of dream:—See how the
> sleeping outflung hand, touching the bedside candle, remembers pain,
> springs back and free while mind and brain sleep on and only make of
> this adjacent heat some trashy myth of reality's escape. [143]

The "*escape*" is ambiguously from, or of, "*reality*," and once again the calculations of a desiring self are referentially "*trashy*." Elsewhere changes not only of self but of plot are sudden, metamorphic, leaving "nothing," since they are burdened with only the "accumulated rubbish-years which we call memory, the recognizable *I*" (196); history operates like the white master whose black butler turned away the boy

Sutpen, provoking a yearning of self to leave some mark against oblivion—a deed, name, house, or tombstone. The mark may seem to have an economy: Sutpen and others affronted, cast aside, or left anonymous are impelled toward a compensatory revenge, if never quite "justice." As Faulkner explained:

> [Sutpen] wanted revenge as he saw it, but also he wanted to establish the fact that man is immortal. . . . He violated all the rules of decency and honor and pity and compassion, and the fates took revenge on him. . . . He wanted a son. . . , and he got too many sons—his sons destroyed one another and then him. He was left with—the only son he had left was a Negro.[29]

Notice the possible slip: Sutpen *was left with a Negro, not a son.* The hesitation, moreover, is inscribed in draft revisions:[30] details were added about how the Sutpen genealogical (non-)-line "ends" with the idiot Jim Bond: "there was nothing left now, nothing out there now but that idiot boy to lurk around those ashes and those four gutted chimneys and howl" (376). Bon's idiocy might perhaps be read as lending support not only to Sutpen's and Henry's fear of miscegenation but to the oppositional rankings (master/slave, white/black) under interrogation. If we were to ask, then, how the interrogation is performed, the question may be met as Thomas Sutpen met certain questions put to him, telling "nothing whatever as pleasantly and courteously as a hotel clerk" (34), for the question and any "matching" answer in turn are likely to be bounded by questionable presuppositions.

An impulse for questioning, even so, if not exactly the same questioning, is notable from the story's outset. Quentin

---

[29]In *Faulkner in the University*, ed. J. Blotner and F. L. Gwynn (Charlottesville: University of Virginia Press, 1959), p. 35.

[30]See Gerald Langford, *Faulkner's Revision of "Absalom, Absalom!"* (Austin: University of Texas Press, 1971), pp. 40–42, 356–62.

is commissioned to hear and tell Miss Rosa's story, but he cannot fathom why; the situation thus is "rhetorical" or uselessly epistemological. Quentin may desire to get "behind" the story to its motivations and to the events surrounding them, but any such movement is blocked, since the signifiers of telling conjure up signifieds (13), which in turn—as signifiers—only reiterate and intensify the problem. Such a situation is itself conscripted as a rhetorical tool: recall Miss Rosa's repeated paralipsis, "I don't plead youth, . . . I don't plead propinquity. . . . And most of all, I do not plead myself" (18–19). Since nothing here that can be made out as a cause will be permitted to explain her plight, Miss Rosa is at once using and undoing any signs that might "work."

She of course in a sense pleads all the factors she mentions even as she explicitly excludes them from being satisfactory; the denials put off (even as they indulge) desires, and just what Miss Rosa will explicitly plead might have to wait, apparently, until she certifies her identity by voicing an opposition—still—to Thomas Sutpen's lack of lineage, origins, or known purposes:

> [He] rode into town out of nowhere with a horse and two pistols and a herd of wild beasts. . . . Anyone could have looked at him once and known that he would be lying about who and where he came from by the very fact that apparently he had to refuse to say at all. And the very fact that he had to choose respectability to hide behind was proof enough (if anyone needed further proof) that what he fled from must have been some opposite of respectability too dark to talk about. [16, 17]

Miss Rosa needs to retain binaries, yet the ostensible "opposite of respectability" is "dark" in a sense beyond sense; like the "wild beasts," it cannot be talked about in detail, and forensically Miss Rosa's "proof" is no proof, since to be silent is not even to lie.

This lack of proof is to be noticed in a text where legalisms and lawyers appear at every turn;[31] Rosa "holds no brief," she has no argument or only has one that is impressive because she has no plaint other than a collection of fragments, glimpses, or contradictions: "I saw Judith's marriage forbidden without rhyme or reason or shadow or excuse; . . . I saw Henry repudiate his home and birthright and then return and practically fling the bloody corpse of his sister's sweetheart at the hem of her wedding gown" (18). Events so stated, if no brief, are no story either, and indeed may undercut narrative linearity by giving away climaxes. Such a situation, however, may itself become a "story": causality, calculation, sequence, legality, morality, all do not "work," which is not quite nothing, since the nonworking works, so to speak, in a sameness without identity, a miscegenation threatened and already, in some Sutpen offspring, instanced.

If so, any sort of genealogical speculation may be relevant. Although Quentin will persist, as if to avoid filiations, in correcting Shreve's mistaking of "Aunt Rosa" for "Miss Rosa," the father surmises regarding Quentin's grandfather's friendship with Sutpen that "maybe she considers you partly responsible through heredity for what happened to her and her family through him" (13). Responsibility so-called can be troped backward, with heredity hardly distinguishable from inheritance; there can be no way, then, to disentangle environment (or "selves") from self, or to discharge debts that are improper or not one's own. Here as elsewhere (in other fathers, sons, siblings, masters), how, as Derrida asks, discharge the debt of the other lodged in oneself and returning

[31]See Marvin K. Singleton, "Personae at Law and in Equity: The Unity of Faulkner's *Absalom, Absalom!*," *Papers on Language and Literature* 3 (1967):354–70.

to oneself "according to a filiation which has not begun to be thought out?"[32] And how speculate on such a debt?

IV

From an "external" situation, on the one hand, such as the town's, any acquaintance with Sutpen and his kin must be *doxa* or even less: "face and horse that none of them had ever seen before, name that none of them had ever heard, and origin and purpose which some of them were never to learn" (32). The community finds itself threatened in Sutpen's marriage of sham propriety and in his slaves "more deadly than any beast" (38); it develops "an acute state of indigestion" and is suspicious of "a nigger in the woodpile somewhere" (46, 72). On the other hand, even when the plot moves toward apparently more assured speculation about Sutpen's so-called origins or purpose, the ostensibly more "internal" situation is still always *doxa*, and external. Most readings of *Absalom, Absalom!* claim, with some justification, that although the story's events are seen from the tellers' conflicting points of view, the relatively most complete telling is performed collaboratively in the concluding version of Quentin and Shreve. Sutpen's project, however, even when narrated as conscious or "internal" intention, is, Cartesianly, always off the mark, confronted with mere mirroring—the boy at the door, the face of itself. The last telling, in other words, like others, is marked by a recurrent, apparently unavoidable dehiscence: the (non-)figure of Charles Bon.

If indeed we review the various tellings, we find that if "Bon" plays a key role in all of them, he is always only what is projected. Mr. Compson's version of the Bon-Henry relation for instance is anything but clear: Bon, indifferent for long to Judith yet murdered to "save" her, acts "as though as a man he did not exist at all": he seems to produce strong ef-

[32]Derrida, *La carte postale*, p. 281.

fects that nonetheless are not "his"; he cannot be linked to them as agent or cause (107, 120, 121), and so "we" are left with mere signifiers—"just the words, the symbols, the shapes themselves" (101).

Although Mr. Compson, who makes this latter statement, discredits thereby his telling in chapter 4, the telling nonetheless leaves impressions, for it in effect prepares for Miss Rosa's in chapter 5 where "conscious" vectors are intensified even though each becomes more nonoppositional or disjunct: a dread of taboos is hysterical but Bon is separated from them. Knowing little more of "Bon" than his name as "Good" (148), Rosa is attracted to the very figure with whom the breaking of taboos had just been associated. A conflict operates, if at all then, surreptitiously—"we" (but not Miss Rosa) are familiar with Mr. Compson's narrative, and so the barrier between her and Bon becomes other than she knows.

Even our awareness of this, however, is no doubt displaced by further negations "of" Bon, who again is not: *"he had been in my house once, . . . and I was not home"* (146). If the house is an image of self and stability, Rosa is absent and Bon's "effect" conjectural in and as dreams: *"there must have been some seed he left"* (146). Rosa's desperate trip to decipher Wash Jones's brief announcement of a killing is ambiguously to be present at an event or to find presence for her *"vacant fairy-tale"* (133, 146). In any case, her headlong rush into Sutpen's house is blocked by "causes" that are all too many: *"the face stopping me dead,"* a *"black arresting and untimorous hand,"* *"Judith standing before the closed door,"* or perhaps the running itself, which began five years ago, *"since he had been in my house too, and had left no more trace than he had left in Ellen's"* (137, 139, 142, 149). The last-stated but prior and ostensibly more motivating cause (in *"since"*) is also *"no trace"* (Derrideanly, "trace"): "Bon" never *is* but always *"was"* or *"was not"* (152); as the nonproductive producer of differences (conflicts, killings), he can never be reported, exposed,

told (*exposé*) as substance or subject, and is not even dissimulating or self-concealing (though for awhile Mr. Compson
and Rosa wish otherwise; 100, 147) in the occult of a not-
knowing.[33] The occurrences of Bon "*stop us dead as though by
some impalpable intervention*" or "*are*" not except as "*echo*," an
"*aftermath*"—in Freud's term, *nachträglich*—and Bon killed is
"*not once mentioned*" (151, 150, 158), for which there may be
"reasons," though perhaps as cryptic as the dialogue:

> *Now you cant marry him.*
> *Why cant I marry him?*
> *Because he's dead.*
> *Dead.*
> *Yes. I killed him.* [172]

The moment of sharpest difference here abolishes differences (in "a terrific, almost unbearable similarity"; 172),
along with communication or conclusion.

V

As if in resistance to such an impasse, Quentin and other
tellers presume, albeit uneasily, that the presence deferred
by signifiers may eventually be appropriated. The very elab-
orateness of Miss Rosa's deferral both dims and intensifies
her hopes, and Quentin eventually learns that she is calling
upon him to find a concealed presence:

> "There is something living in that house."
> "In that house? It's Clytie. Dont she—"
> "No. Something living in it. Hidden in it." [172]

[33]Derrida, "Différance," in *Marges de la philosophie* (Paris: Minuit, 1972),
p. 6: "Reserving and not showing itself, [*différance*] exceeds . . . the order of
truth, without moreover dissimulating itself as something, as a mysterious
being, in the occult of a not-knowing [*comme un étant mystérieux, dans l'occulte
d'un non-savoir*]" (my translation).

Quentin's and Rosa's visit, however, is itself deferred by tellings that lead up to, and parallel, the outcome. For when
Quentin and Shreve in chapter 6 and thereafter construct
their narrative, which imaginarily "explains," they do so by
recuperating the classical sign—that is, by attempting to
make "Bon" (the enigmatic absence in prior versions) into a
subjectivity and by linking him to otherwise incoherent effects. Since they also depict Bon as a crazed seeker of paternal presence, they move, in ostensible totalization, toward
apparent "origins" in Sutpen himself as consciousness or
teller.

Consider their strategies. The narrators, on Grandfather's
testimony, offer to depict Sutpen's earliest years: "innocence" in Sutpen lingers on from a prelapsarian childhood
where "the land belonged to . . . everybody" (221). The fall
into knowledge is problematic, however, since the very example of innocence is suspect ("the only colored people were
Indians and you only looked down at them over your rifle
sights"; 221) and since Sutpen learns in (or after?) his innocence that there is a "difference not only between white men
and black ones, but . . . between white men and white men,
not to be measured by lifting anvils or gouging eyes" (226).
Although he struggles against the white-white or nondiffer-
ent difference, Sutpen has difficulty distinguishing himself:
he does not know when he was born nor "where he had
come from nor where he was nor why" (264, 227; cf. 220), a
not-knowing that in effect calls into question not only his efforts but those of the tellers, who must use other than bio-
graphical strategies to disclose possible signifieds.

Quentin and Shreve thus mediate the Sutpen-Bon "relation" above all in images of face, or in encounters face-to-
face. This, to be sure, is traditional enough: in biblical and
Augustinian texts, the face is an idealized (if therefore pecul-
iarly troublesome) sign: more than other signifiers it "must,"
if alive, have consciousness connected with it, revealing a self

that is meaningfully different yet minimally deferred. In *Absalom, Absalom!* it is nonetheless precisely the Sutpen face that cancels differences and blocks intersubjectivity. With eyes "like pieces of a broken plate," the face is a barrier; the "ogre-face" is "like the mask in Greek tragedy," and Ellen, marrying, is "transmogrified into a mask" (45, 62, 60). When Rosa runs into Sutpen's house, she mistakes the fact that stops her—it is *"not Henry's face, . . . Sutpen face enough, but not his"* (136): the children replicate a masklike face of no emotions, a face that despite differences in color, sex, or age is the same in its impenetrability (182, 201, 277, 317, 329).

In the Bible, the sight of King David's face was a sign of welcome and its concealment, of disapproval (2 Sam. 3:13). Absalom banished "returned to his own house and saw not the king's face," though when he was mistakenly killed, "the king covered his face, and the king cried with a loud voice, O my son Absalom; O Absalom, my son, my son!" (2 Sam. 14:24, 19:4; King James version). If King David hid his face in mourning and lamented, Sutpen does not, since his face, even uncovered, is covered: Bon hopes that he need only see Sutpen's face, and "there would be that flash, . . . and he would know for sure and forever" (319). Here again, however, possible signifieds are always only empty signifiers: he "saw face to face the man who might be his father, and nothing happened" (320). He waits, and "still no sign," asking at the war's end, *"And he sent me no word?"* (321, 356). If the expectation is logocentric, however, from and for whom in *Absalom, Absalom!* is conclusive word ever sent? The quest for presence by Bon and indeed by the narrators can, in other words, be read as a thematization, but since the quest proves impossible, it may also allegorize the impossibility of reading.

The father's crucial logocentric dream is for instance rather cryptic: his descendants are to be "born without even having to know that they were once riven forever free from brutehood" (261). Classically, only the *logos* is subject to proper mimesis—the bestial can only be aped; animals lack speech, and their sounds of behavior are disbarred from truly "human" affairs.[34] What is insidious about Bon is his mirroring back, as earlier noted, of what is projected; Henry (in Mr. Compson's version) "aped [Bon's] clothing and manner and . . . his manner of living." Note "aped" (96, also 102, 107; cf. "ape-like," 205, 206): when Bon, according to this account, tries to persuade Henry that his (Bon's) relationship with an octoroon woman should pose no obstacle to marriage with Henry's sister Judith, Henry feels drawn into some sort of imperceptible corruption involving taboos of Negro blood; Bon's attempted—and resisted—"trump" (118; cf. 277) is that "this woman, this child, are niggers," and although that, for Henry, "is not right," Henry identifies with Bon, and by mimesis or "metamorphosis"—with its overtones of bestial transformation—can commit "the pure and perfect incest" (118, 96–97).

Mimesis, it seems, cannot quite be separated from incest, "aping," or partly unknown and terrifying contamination. If for instance Sutpen's naked Haitian slaves are especially "wild" and their language is unknown, Sutpen would like to presume himself all the more archly "opposite" them, partly owing to sheer physical "white" will but also (paradoxically) to his cross-breeding them not only with domesticated American slaves but perhaps even with himself (85). The operations of dominating and separating are perilously intertwined; conscious mastery is subverted in deferred or unconscious "results." Thus in Sutpen's fighting off blacks in the Haitian rebellion, "a shadow that almost emerged for a moment and then faded again" is a girl (247, 249, 240). Sutpen is a virgin at this point, and "that too was a part of

---

[34]Derrida, "White Mythology," trans. F. T. C. Moore, *NLH* 4 (1974):37–39. ". . . *Mimesis* so defined [by Aristotle] belongs to the *logos* and is not a matter of aping [*singerie*] and mimicking, of animal gesture; it is connected with the possibility of truth in discourse" (37); *Marges*, p. 282.

the design" (248); he knows nothing except that the girl seems on "his" side within the barricaded house and that the black rebellion threatens to contaminate unknowably his sexuality;[35] indeed as protection and almost part of the struggle, Sutpen marries (254, 255). This marriage-as-protection, though, is to prove adverse; Sutpen believed "that darkness was merely something you saw, or could not see in; overseeing what he oversaw and not knowing that he was overseeing it" (251–52). "Overseeing" is a double registration as pun: Sutpen hunts "the half-breed" for two days only to find "the body of" one of them "without even knowing that what he was meeting was a blank wall of black secret faces" (252), and the struggle he though he fought and won he was all the while losing.

A powerful social-sexual threat, the "nigger" (if "outside" the *logos*) must not to be spoken to but only commanded or forced: Sutpen as "nigger" is ordered away from a white door without a chance to speak, and Charles Bon as "nigger" need be sent no word, "*just warned*" (237, 349). Sutpen "knows" perhaps for some such reason that "they (the niggers) are not it, not what you wanted to hit" (230), though "what" he might want to hit—the nonoriginary "producer" of differences—can never be present or known, a condition so to speak incarnated in the inscrutable half-breeds to all appearances white, mocking in effect the flimsy legalisms "which declare that one eighth of a specified kind of blood shall outweigh seven eight[h]s of another kind" (115). In the disseminating double plot, Sutpen's unspoken horror of the half-breed cannot (any more than the half-breed as "trace") be known or controlled by some calculable binary opposite.

[35]Cf. Paul Ricoeur, *The Symbolism of Evil*, trans. E. Buchanan (Boston: Beacon, 1969), pp. 25–26: "What resists reflection is the idea of a quasi-material something that infects as a sort of filth, that harms by invisible properties, and that nevertheless works in the manner of a force in our individedly psychic and corporeal existence."

Sutpen searches with the help of Grandfather's "legal mind" to find where he made the "mistake," but this simply re-tropes his earlier condition of having nothing "to measure it by" (273, 233). We cannot but notice the self-assuming meta-physics by which a review of "logical steps," if performed with diligent "alertness," will exhaust the field of possibili-ties: like the Cartesian narrator of the *Discourse on Method*, who also urged reviews, Sutpen is certain that any "error" temporarily overseen can, upon scrutiny, be disclosed and corrected (53, 267–86).

Sutpen would thus like the line of valid deduction to be conflated with the line of self-styled "proper" breeding. In-stead, however, his descendants "are" not (have no origins in) a sanctionable line, though precisely in that they resem-ble him. The supposedly miscegenated and "therefore" non-existent son with a nonfather and nonproper name himself fathers another, Charles Etienne St. Valéry, acting (like "Bon" and "the demon") apart from namable connections: "saying nothing, refusing to speak at all, sitting there in court sullen, pale and silent: so at this point all truth, evi-dence vanished into a moiling clump of negro[es] . . . . There had been no cause, no reasons for it; none to know exactly what happened" (202). The traditional Southern rhetoric by which the two races are placed and then praised (for "pride and integrity and forbearance") is shaken by an unidentifiable figure, and the forensic voice must somehow come to a stop:

> . . . and it [was] already too late, as if Hamblett's [the ora-tor's] own voice had waked him at last or as if someone had snapped his fingers under his nose and waked him, he looking at the prisoner now but saying "white" again even while his voice died away as if the order to stop the voice had been shocked into a short circuit, and every face in the room turned toward the prisoner as Hamblett cried, *"What are you? Who and where did you come from?"* [203; cf. 32, 48, 93]

Let us recapitulate: Bon and his descendants, as the re-pressed plot of and against Sutpen's, are not simply opposite the system that would place them. They are unassimilable remainders; they are equations that only oddly equate ("you give me two and two and . . . it make[s] five"; 118). Selves indeterminately merge with and duplicate others, and darkness as boundary for socially defined humanity is tenuous in relation to the (non-) results of sexual impulse. Does Sutpen, for all his care in breeding, produce a proper mimesis of himself? And is the father inevitably a nonfather if his engendering is not what he considers proper? Is there, again, any analogy to Sutpen's breeding in the efforts of the Compson father and son to shape a narrative in which repetitions of identical phrases in "different" situations (234, 339) may partially erase the very meanings being stressed? Is there indeed even a propriety, as we might be tempted to believe, in what Sutpen considers to be the nonpropriety of his offspring?

The Bon (non-)line can nowhere, it seems, be contained. The "white-colored" Charles-Etienne, who slings his wife's "ape-like body" into the faces of blacks and whites alike, is unwilling to conceal yet unable to reveal "what" he is: "negro[es] . . . thought he was a white man and believed it only the more strongly when he denied it; the white men, when he said he was a negro, believed that he lied in order to save his skin, or worse" (206). Here and more so with Jim Bond, genealogical and social indifference is beyond the regime of concealment and presence ("*I dont even know whether he wants to hide it or not*"; 204); Bon's son will answer neither to filial connections nor to Grandfather's proposals that he make a new beginning (203–4), and Bond "wouldn't have cared" or known about his name or ancestry: "if you had told him . . . , it would have touched and then vanished from what

you (not he) would have had to call his mind long before it
could have set up any reaction at all, either of pride or pleasure, anger or grief" (215). Precisely in lacking what the narrators "(not he) would have had to call his mind," Bond
eludes the story that would reach its "end" in him, whose so-
called idiocy is a function of the tellers' "shrewdness" (cf.
273, 156–57).

Shreve's remark, that "it takes two niggers to get rid of
one Sutpen" (378), is a *reductio* of the ratiocination (280), the
shrewdness by which Bond or a dying Henry is the "just"
sign of Sutpen's ruin or by which Miss Rosa could say to
Bond, "You aint any Sutpen!" (371). As Quentin (or the
land) almost told Miss Rosa on her penultimate trip to Sutpen's house, *"you will find no destination but . . . merely . . .
harmless and inscrutable night"* (175). Neither something nor
nothing, Bond both is and undoes the Sutpen design, which
in any origins or results had repeatedly "vanished and left
no trace, nothing," "coming down like it had been built out
of smoke" (238, 241, 267). Bond, except for the narrators, is
not "no nothing in the . . . slack-mouthed idiot face" and
surely not "the scion, the heir, the apparent (though not obvious)"; half-breed or trace, "he didn't seem to ever get any
further away but they couldn't get any nearer" (370, 376).

If the Faulknerian text thus confounds conventional mea-
sures for social planning or critique, it does so as double
writing. The social hegemony's pressure to retain black/
white and white/white oppositions (of all sorts) becomes as
striking as its monstrousness construed as systematic exclu-
sions of the other as, uncontrollably, what it constructed as
itself. We noticed such a situation in the Augustinian conversion, the Quixotic Cogito, and the Shandean changeling.
They and the Faulknerian instance might be used to recall
(at a point respectful of conclusions) our prefatory image of
deconstruction attendant at a slow, monstrous birth.

7

Epilogue

> This problem of reading cannot be displayed, except in a family scene.
>
> —Derrida, *Glas*

Instances of monstrosity or aberration have been remarked often in the preceding pages, and not without consequences for the question of authority. Literary and philosophical texts traditionally assume, after all, the possibility of an identifying or authorizing gesture: the father or author as on "I" is endowed with powers that are representative or generate some legitimate line. In self-questioning narratives, however, genealogy cannot begin with the father. Take this in several ways at least: the crucial agency never seems to have made a beginning (with the maternal, the material), never was his own beginning, may have conceived, but unsatisfactorily, the offspring marking only hiatus or dilution, if that. And so there arises a problem as to how the subsequent "family"—genealogy, story—is to be read.

The text even of St. Augustine does not escape such a problem. By Christian doctrine the Son in the resurrection returns to the Father, and his followers, with the eucharist, return in turn to him. None of these (re-)turns, paradoxically, is to be taken tropologically, for to take them as rhetoric or figure is to take them without their proper force, which needs no help from rhetoric (it was precisely "rhetoric" indeed which the converted Augustine relinquished). Thus although postconversation language in the *Confessions* is hardly nontropological, we might be wary even so of presuming that what seem to be the earliest problems of the *Confessions* are still at the end "the same" ones. Nor can we presume on the other hand that if we attend quietly to Augustine's words, as he did to Ambrose's, we will automatically be granted some insight; the Augustinian text in its very intimacy may exclude its readers, or some of them. This cannot itself be read, however, as a sure sign of Augustine's proximity to God, for not only do signs remain of the narrator's continuing isolation, but signs in the *Confessions* are patently, and possibly thematically, always signs of the sign; even the angels merely read God's face, and if the Son *is* the Father, Augustine is not, except perhaps very indirectly, the Son. Doctrinally, what the Father is supposed to do (with the Son's return to him or with his followers' eucharistic consummations) is to make the sign disappear into full presence. Yet before that, and just as doctrinally, God the Father—if only to be recognized as such—needs to go out from himself in a son or sign of himself. The very distance which thus makes fatherhood possible always makes it incomplete.

We need not puzzle over which of these aspects of divine fathering is most comparable to human fathering, since Christian theophany could be called an extended act of self-inscription. Humanly, to the extent that the sign cannot be consumed into full presence, the father provides a name, legitimizes signs or offspring, placing them properly or referentially—though frequently, we have discovered, in conjunction with a filiative background that threatens perpetually to undo efforts of adequate nomination. The supposedly monstrous sons of *Tristram Shandy* and *Absalom, Absalom!* make the fathers as monstrous as the fathers make the sons—a series of mutual reflections that are never simply representations or appropriations. This difficult situation is most poignant when the family's so-called insider starts or ends up on the so-called outside, the outsider on the inside, or the boundaries seem blurred.

The situation, moreover, is only slightly less acute in texts in which the narrators attempt, Cartesianly, to become their own fathers. We noticed at the outset that the problems of Cartesian narrative have come to prevail over those of genealogical narrative, but we might also notice that what could be called the rhetoric of readability is always in a certain sense familial or pseudofamilial. For instance the solitary narrator of the *Meditations* sits comfortably by his fire, with a piece of beeswax from his own garden, and we are apparently asked to make ourselves at home, possibly even to act as his family. Such a domestic scene, if it seems to nurture readability, also stages reading's problem: if we have to be "at home" in our reading, might not that itself promote something less than the scrupulous doubting which the narrator requires? If on the other hand we resist Cartesian requirement, is the Cogito on that account any more or less self-fathering in his self-representation?

This question of self-fathering and the domestic or (pseudo)familial is explicitly thematized with Don Quixote, we might notice, who not only strongly misreads but begins and ends in proximity to what might be called, weakly, his family. That family of course "understands" his insanity, which is a matter of reading texts, but the readings and counterreadings of texts involve not merely sanity but strong and violent desire, as in *quaero* or question. The family is where desire typically takes place (in complexes and romances), but the domesticators here are not his family (most are not of kin), and the prologue author can but doubtfully postulate family resemblances to Don Quixote.

Similarly doubtful postulations marked the ostensibly more familial fiction of *Tristram Shandy* and *Absalom, Absalom!* As in *Don Quixote*, the "end" of substitutive doublings is questionable: the protagonist may seem to approach his proper self but no longer has a self, since the end collapses the doubleness (of reading, seeing, doing) that had been the enabling play both of and against signifying. Only the unappropriated aberration, it seems, can function as reading's spur.

Index

Index

Index

Library of Congress Cataloging in Publication Data

Flores, Ralph.
   The rhetoric of doubtful authority.

   Includes index.
    1. Deconstruction. 2. Authority in literature. I. Title.
PN98.D43F4   1984   801'.95   83-15297
ISBN 0-8014-1625-6